DESIGNING
CONNECTED
CONTENT

PLAN AND MODEL DIGITAL PRODUCTS
FOR TODAY AND TOMORROW

MIKE ATHERTON
CARRIE HANE

DESIGNING CONNECTED CONTENT
Plan and Model Digital Products for Today and Tomorrow

Mike Atherton and Carrie Hane

New Riders
www.newriders.com

New Riders is an imprint of Peachpit, an imprint of Pearson Education, Inc.

To report errors, please send a note to errata@peachpit.com

Executive Editor: Nancy Davis
Development and Project Editor: Robyn G. Thomas
Senior Production Editor: Tracey Croom
Copyeditor: Scout Festa
Proofreader: Kim Wimpsett
Tech Editors: Marli Mesibov and Paul Rissen
Compositor: Kim Scott, Bumpy Design
Indexer: Rebecca Plunkett
Cover Design: Chuti Prasertsith
Interior Design: Kim Scott, Bumpy Design

ISBN 13: 978-0-13-476338-5
ISBN 10:   0-13-476338-6

1 17

To Ryan and Adam,
I hope you dance.

To Miranda,
Your future is whatever you design.

ACKNOWLEDGMENTS

We feel like Academy Award winners, getting to thank people who got us here. But there's no way we could have done it by ourselves. And our thanks go to...

Jonathan Colman, **Jessica DuVerneay**, and **Annette Priest** for reviewing our early proposal to see if we were really onto something new and different. And if it made sense to anyone but us.

Marli Mesibov for first bringing back-end content strategy to *UX Booth* and also being a fantastic technical editor, always making sure we saw a different point of view.

Paul Rissen for so many things. A BBC conspirator, lead information architect on the IA Summit team, and technical editor extraordinaire, you made sure we got the modeling, structure, and URL stuff right. Please write your own book soon!

IA Summit 2015 team—**Jessica DuVerneay**, **Veronica Erb**, **Jon Hadden**, **Stéphane Corlosquet**, and **Jeremy Burton**. Without your work and your belief in the vision and process, none of this would be possible.

Abby Covert and **Lou Rosenfeld** for pushing us to write a book about domain modeling.

None of this would be possible without our editors at Pearson. **Nancy Davis**, our executive editor, for her excitement and encouragement every step of the way. **Robyn Thomas**, our development editor, for her patience, understanding, and momentum. We never met a deadline we didn't like.

And the rest of the content strategy, information architecture, and user experience design communities. You keep us honest. You keep us learning. You keep us here.

Carrie thanks...

Krystee Dryer and **Asea Ginsburg** for teaching me all about Drupal and design, respectively, and for accepting content strategy into your work. And to all our colleagues at Balance Interactive who helped create a content-first process that has held strong across teams and time. Asea, you always knew I'd do this one day! I'll never forget that. Спасибо.

Ryan and Adam Dennison for putting up with me while I did this. Thank you from the bottom of my heart for your patience and help. You're the best kids this mom could ask for!

My parents, **Sue Hane** and **Paul Hane**. Thank you for believing in me and never holding me back. And **Tracie Varitek,** the little sister who never let me get away with anything. You're always part of my story.

All my teachers, classmates, teammates, coaches, colleagues, family, and friends who challenged, encouraged, and supported me in some way big or small throughout life. Especially **Ardith Laskowski,** "Mrs. L," my elementary school librarian, who first cultivated my love for books and organizing them.

And **Mike,** you started this story long ago and got me thinking about structured content and modeling with "Beyond the Polar Bear." Thanks for letting me add some plot points. We did it! You'll have to endure my strategic nagging no more.

Mike thanks...

Michael Smethurst and **Silver Oliver** for showing me there was more beyond the polar bear and helping me see a different way of connecting the world. You're the real brains of this operation; I just make the slides.

Tom Scott, Chris Sizemore, Yves Raimond, and the rest of the BBC "coalition of the willing," past and present. Your efforts over the years have shown how new ideas can seep into old corporations. Thank you for giving me new things to talk about.

Vanessa Foss and **Dick Hill,** formerly of ASIS&T, for organizing the IA Summit conference that provided me with a community and a professional network.

Alicia Dougherty-Wold for giving me the space to be 43, an author, and a Facebook content strategist all at the same time.

To all the huckleberry friends who've suffered with me through some or all of this journey. You know who you are. Especially you. Maybe I'll shut up about the damn book now.

And to **Carrie,** who wrote her acknowledgments first, so now I feel guilty. Thank you for your encouragement, your questioning, and your energy. And for letting me keep some of the dad jokes.

CONTENTS

Foreword xi

Introduction xiii

LET'S GET CONNECTED

1   **Designing From the Bottom Up**   **3**

New Model Army 4

Structure Connects Content 4

It's Design All the Way Down 9

Chapter by Chapter 12

Climbing the Summit. 14

2   **Why We Need a New Way of Approaching Digital Content**   **17**

Does This Sound Familiar?. 18

Take a Step Back. 19

A New Approach. 20

3   **Understanding Structured Content**   **31**

Setting Content Free. 32

What Is Structured Content?. 32

Moving Toward Structured Content. 34

Using Structured Content 38

Go Forth and Create Structure 42

STRUCTURING CONTENT

4   **Researching the Subject Domain**   **45**

Where Do We Begin? 46

Deconstructing Subjects 46

Getting Started 50

Talking to the Users 59

Overcoming Objections 61

Defining Problems Before Solutions 64

5 Creating a Domain Model   **67**

How Do We Make the Connections?......................68

Connecting Concepts.................................68

Forming Meaningful Relationships.....................71

Breaking Down a Model 72

Modeling Is Teamwork 74

Using the Sticky Note Method 74

Agreeing on Your Domain............................76

Finding a Ubiquitous Language.......................80

Establishing Cardinality.............................80

Knowing When to Stop 84

Bringing In Experts 85

Who Uses the Model?................................87

More Examples.....................................88

Modeling for the Future.............................91

6 Translating to a Content Model   **97**

Content vs. Expression 98

From Domain Model to Content Model 98

From Objects to Content Types........................102

Reconnecting to Form the Content Model...............110

How the Content Model Is Used 111

PUBLISHING CONTENT

7 Designing Connected Content   **117**

UX for Content 118

Constructing Content Resources 120

Prepare Your Content...............................132

Filling In the Blanks 137

Content First, Content Only..........................140

8 Implementing Connected Content   **141**

From Theory to Reality 142

Content Management and the CMS 142

Content Types—The Technical Side 148

Taxonomy—A Quick Note 157
Content Creation. 159
Assemble the Implementation Team 162
Everything Is Connected 165

9   Bringing Your Content to Life   167
Designing with Content. 168
Planning Your Templates 171
Designing Templates 174
Designing Navigation 185
Being Everywhere 194
Stable Structure, Creative Content. 197
Looking Back 198

THE FUTURE

10   The Future Isn't Waiting   201
Real Talk 202
Convincing Your Boss 204
Making This Happen 206
Measuring Success. 207
It's Just Information Architecture 208
Linking Data 209
What's Next? 210

Index 213

FOREWORD

YOUR CONTENT IS PROBABLY CRAP.

In 1951, science-fiction author Theodore Sturgeon gave a lecture at New York University. During the audience Q&A he responded to a remark that the majority of science fiction is terrible by saying "90 percent of everything is crap."

Rather than refuting the point being made, he made the claim that science fiction is really no different than any other genre in terms of the prevalence of low-quality examples. This point has become known as Sturgeon's law or Sturgeon's revelation.

Before going any further, I have some bad news. Based on Sturgeon's law, there is a 90 percent chance that whatever content you are working on is crap.

Here's the good news. If you are reading this foreword, it means you found this book. Within these pages you will gain the knowledge that you need to make your content a lot less crappy.

When the authors of this book started talking about content modeling at information architecture and user experience conferences, it was like a breath of fresh air. Our community had focused for too long on the classification of content without consideration for the structure of the content itself and the useful relationships between individual pieces of content that were possible by looking past simple hierarchies. Our overly classification-centric view on digital content meant that Sturgeon's law actually underestimated the amount of crap out there.

My hope is that this book is the first of many steps that our community can take toward improving the way the world creates and consumes digital content. I can't think of two people better suited to the task than Carrie and Mike. Over the years they have tirelessly educated people in workshops and conference talks about the value that content modeling can provide. I am thrilled that they have finally sat down and put these lessons into a referenceable source.

I can assure you that this book is one of the 10 percent.

—Abby Covert
  Author, *How to Make Sense of Any Mess*

INTRODUCTION

Hey, thanks for buying this book.

And if you're reading the free preview on Amazon, thanks also to you—you're illustrating what this book is about: how content created just once can be structured and connected to appear all over the place. But also you should totally buy the whole book.

HOW IS THIS A THING?

Indulge us while we tell you about people you've never heard of in a story that goes nowhere. Alternatively, call your mother. Back in 2011, Mike spoke at the Information Architecture Summit about how the BBC was doing a little remodeling of its digital publishing strategy to help people find and explore more world-class BBC content. The talk went down pretty well. It gave an overview of building content structures based on a subject domain (Google "Beyond the Polar Bear" to spend 45 minutes of your life that you'll never get back). But it had a missing link: how to go from abstract models to the nuts-and-bolts of content publishing.

In the audience for that talk was Carrie, who was coming at large-scale content publishing challenges from a different angle. As a consultant, she'd been helping clients set up their publishing pipelines in a way that best suited the shape of the content. We saw an obvious connection and found a way to make our pieces fit. Together we had the elements of a full-spectrum process that begins with researching your subject and follows right through to publishing content... well, wherever you want. As fate decreed, we would put this process through its paces for the same conference where we met.

Throughout this book you'll hear all about our work on the 2015 IA Summit, some of the mistakes we made, and what we learned as a result. Since that time, we've refined the process and the way we explain it. And each time we've explained it, in the limited space allowed by lectures and workshops, people have told us, "You should really write a book." You're welcome.

WHY WE WROTE
DESIGNING CONNECTED CONTENT

As with many digital disrupters who proclaim the death of old media paradigms, what we really wanted was a book deal. Not for the fortune and glory, you understand. Nor to wax lyrical as the leading brainiacs in this subject. Because we're really not—though we're lucky to count as friends and advisors some of the true pioneers. (And believe us—if you want to find out how little you really understand something, try writing a book about it.)

No, we wrote this because we've found a way of working that addresses many of the problems faced by content practitioners like us. We've found success in taking ideas that look pretty technical and presenting them in a way that's a little less mystical and scary. Mostly we wrote it because we think this connected content stuff is cool, and we want you to think it's cool too.

For a long time, digital publishing was synonymous with "web design," with projects focused on visuals and modes of interaction. Content got lost in the mix. Later the practice of "content strategy" shone a spotlight on the need to plan the process and purpose for content, rather than vomiting a load of old garbage onto the internet. Yet the folks we know in the content field often tell us that while they're rocking the creation of useful and usable content, it's a challenge to know how that content should be classified and organized. In several cases, they don't even have a hand in the presentation of the content they've made.

We want that to change. Making content make sense isn't just about the words on the page. Understanding comes from making the connections between one topic and the next. There's content in the context. So if you're in the business of making or publishing digital content, we want to offer you some tools that may help.

Over the past decade, we've begged, borrowed, and stolen the following from the best: a clear approach to determining which content to publish. Collaborative exercises to expose a natural content structure. And a development pipeline that drives content and all its connections to many places at once. We've remixed it into a process that's worked for us. It's a little bit technical. But not very scary.

WHO ARE YOU, ANYWAY?

But enough about us, let's do you. Your organization, or maybe your client, has a communications problem to solve. And somehow the responsibility for the design and management of digital content has landed on your shoulders. You're the content strategist. The content marketer. Maybe even the communications director or chief content officer. You wrestle with content audits, URL schemas, and a volley of incoming requests that leave you with a large content mess to keep untangled. We're here to help. There's a better way, we promise.

We assume you already have some game in making digital things for other people. And you probably work with folks brandishing a smorgasbord of skills different from your own. We offer you an approach that not only connects your content but helps you connect your team.

The user experience designers on your team are great at crafting environments that make content easy to find and explore. They want to display that content through new or updated interfaces without having to start over every time. We'll show how to inform interface decisions by designing and planning your content before a single pixel is drawn.

Together with your product manager you'll lay the foundations of a multidevice, multiplatform strategy. It's one where content structures map to mental models and accommodate existing and future needs. It's one that allows them to experiment more, iterate easily, and ship faster.

We'll bet the software engineers would like a more active role in the design of the products they're asked to build. They probably want more robust specifications and requirements, instead of being handed an interface wireframe and having to decode its implications. You'll be able to include them in a design process that begins under the hood and anticipates future expansion.

If your organization is grasping for that holy grail of digital transformation, they need to overhaul how they connect to customers. Being digital-first means being content-first. It means reaching customers on every device and every search and social platform with useful information that's less about you and more about them. We'll explore how the routes to content discovery have changed and show you how to maximize production budgets through efficient, reusable information focused on people's needs. Who knows, you might even get them to break the habit of commissioning a new website every three or four years.

THIS BOOK, THEN

While we'll opine muchly on the state of digital content (and the organizations that publish it), what you have here is a "how to" book. We're nothing if not pragmatic and practical, so we wrote a toolkit that you can adapt and apply to your own situation. It's a manual for creating and publishing useful and usable content.

It will show you how to

- Design digital products around content that's based on the needs and understanding of your audience
- Involve stakeholders where they offer the most value (hint: it's their business expertise, not their ability to judge design)
- Plan content and navigation structures that scale without breaking
- Separate content and structure from presentation, making future redesigns cheaper and less painful
- Align your multidisciplinary team on a common vision
- Publish your content to the desktop, mobile, wearable, and screenless devices of today and tomorrow

WHAT THIS BOOK ISN'T

As we'll get into later, something you realize when you explore any topic is how seamlessly and sneakily it connects to many others. Drawing the borders of the map can be difficult. So while we'll drop casual references to various strategies and tactics for content creation and management, we've tried not to drift into tangents.

This book is not

- A beginner's guide to content strategy
- A manual for visual or interaction design
- Tips on improving your grammar, punctuation, and writing style
- A tutorial on metadata schemas or publishing linked data
- Anything directly to do with improving your search rankings or marketing your content

There are far, far better people to guide you through those things. We're grateful to every one of them. And you should totally buy their books too.

HOW TO USE THIS BOOK

Carry it everywhere you go. Study its lovingly crafted words and sage advice. Slip in a bookmark and take it to the park. We spent months writing this damn thing, the least you can do is read it. Just start from here and go all the way through. You'll ace the exam at the end. (There's no exam. But there is an end, mercifully.)

Yeah, no. We certainly don't have the patience to read a whole book when we just want to brush up on a specific tactic, and we imagine you to be just like us. In the first couple of chapters, we'll tell you what's coming up in the book and lay out our argument for why a structured, content-first approach is a good thing. After that, we're into the tactics that take us from research through to publishing. But maybe you're already somewhere along this journey or doing things in a different order. Maybe some of our advice doesn't apply to your situation. Flip through and jump around. What might look like a recipe to be followed in sequence is really a collection of jazz riffs to be improvised upon.

PAY IT FORWARD

When first we latched onto domain-driven, structured content, it was one of those aha moments where we couldn't imagine going back to our old ways of working. We hope you'll feel the same way. Use the ideas in this book to facilitate conversations that get your team on the same page. Discuss, debate, and discover ways of working that help everyone play to their strengths.

Share what you learn with others in your organization and with the community at large. Share with us—we're @carriehd and @mikeatherton on Twitter, for as long as that's still a thing.

We've learned so much from others in the field, and we'd love to learn more from you. Just like the content, we're better when we're connected.

Grab a cuppa and dig in!

Mike & Carrie

LET'S GET CONNECTED

CHAPTER 1

DESIGNING FROM THE BOTTOM UP

"Call me Ishmael," she didn't say. But wouldn't it be a great opening if she had?

In fact it, was "Ashman" she was going by now and would really prefer that her old name weren't plastered all over the schedule. As the digital team for an information architecture conference, who were we to deny our featured speaker such a simple request?

Behind the scenes, conferences are chaos. Herding attendees between sessions and break times. Making sure the keynote speaker resurfaces after last night's opening reception. Answering yet again that yes, there will be gluten-free cupcakes. It may look razzle-dazzle on the front end, but back-stage you're flailing like Kermit, just trying to hold all the crazy together. Really the last thing you need in that moment is to hear that a speaker's name is wrong on the website. And not just on their bio, but on the schedule page too. And the homepage. And not just the website, but the mobile app. And all of the onsite digital displays that timetable the day's events.

"No problem," we said. One simple change, and Dr. Ashman was everywhere.

NEW MODEL ARMY

Content is data.

Sorry to sound so reductive—it is of course art, poetry, music, lively discourse, noble proclamation, informative news, nurturing education, and compelling inspiration. (It's perhaps ironic that some of the people who give it such a catch-all, brand-X commodity name as "content" are the content strategists sworn to protect it.)

But it *is* data, even if you take all the technology away. Content provides information about the world around us. It defines, describes, discusses, and debates things and ideas. Concepts. People. Places. Objects. It furnishes us with fact.

Technology helps, though. Tell a computer some tiny stories about the world around you, and it can figure out how that world fits together. Type someone's name on a web page, and your fellow humans are smart enough to intuit that you're referencing a person. But apply a little metadata structure under the hood to tell your computer that there's this thing called a `Person` and that among their better qualities they have a `First Name` and a `Last Name`. Suddenly that person's name is more than just a dumb string of text. It's a living attribute of a profile record in a machine-readable database. Go on to tell the computer that this `Person` has the role of `Speaker` for a particular `Session` at something called an `Event`. Little by little, the computer starts to make sense of the world. Now it understands that this named person is giving a session (at a particular time and place) within your event. So if you were to, say, update their last name, the computer dutifully knows that the change should happen on that person's profile, their session details and schedule, the list of speakers—in fact anywhere they're referenced at all. A robot army to do your heavy lifting! Content management made easy.

STRUCTURE CONNECTS CONTENT

This book covers our process for planning and designing content as structured data and then publishing that content to different user interfaces. That sounds pretty dry and technical, and let's be frank—later on, we'll ask you to roll up your sleeves and get into structural diagramming that wouldn't look out of place on the desk of a database architect. We're content strategists, but a book on voice and tone this ain't.

As with all technology, the data wrangling is just a means to an end. Structure provides opens pathways to content from all across the web. Structure opens pathways to content from all across the web, making it easier to locate and to consume. Content wants to be used. It's there to meet the needs of its audience. You spend all that time and money creating it because you think it will meet a predefined objective. But first, people have to find it. And when they do, they have to make sense of it. This isn't like the old days, when someone would type your website address into their browser, arrive at your home page, and then descend through your menu trees until, through careful consideration, they arrived at their chosen destination. No, these days people pull out their phone, bash the first thing they can think of into Google, and take advice from one of the top five results. People are arriving straight into the middle of your structure, and they have limited patience to make sense of what they find.

Designing for that behavior means understanding how your audience thinks. We'll come back to this point throughout this book, so we might as well say it first here: people's interest in their subject of choice doesn't begin and end with your content. They've come to look at your stuff because they have a particular itch that needs scratching. Maybe they're looking to buy a house. Or get feeding advice for their new pet iguana. Or relocate to Arizona. Or learn the history of civil rights. Hate to say it, but it's never really about you.

And you can respect that through the way you structure your content. Whatever field you're in, whatever topic you publish content about, figure out how your audience thinks about that topic. What's their mental model? What kinds of things do they consider most useful, and what are those things called? How, in their minds, is one thing related to another?

Design starts from sharing a common language. Information spaces have contextual concepts, relationships, and rules. Structure brings context, and context is how we build understanding. So your most fundamental design is a model of connected concepts within a subject domain. Design your content around their priorities, not yours, and you'll be better positioned to help them achieve their goals and get a decent return on your publishing investment.

START MAKING SENSE WITH STRUCTURE

Structure makes sense. Also, structure *makes* sense. *Sensemaking* is the term used in the information science and human-computer interaction communities for the process by which people give meaning to an experience. It's been described as "fitting data into a mental model, and fitting a frame around the data." That's a pretty good introduction to the design process you'll follow:

1. Research and map out a content structure based on the broad subject area you work within (what we call the *subject domain*—something like personal pensions, medical equipment, or comic book collecting), including how the things in the domain are related.

2. Create content that maps to *examples* of things in that domain. (In comic book collecting, you might have a thing called *Publisher*, of which an example would be *Marvel Comics*.)

3. Design your content management system to support publishing based on the structure you've mapped out.

4. Design interface templates that will bring your content to every device you want to support.

5. Publish! Measure how well your content is performing, and continue to explore new ways to remix and share it. Make plans for the content you'll create next.

If you've worked on a digital product design before, some of this might seem a little topsy-turvy.

You may be accustomed to a practice in which *design* means *interface design* and begins with sketching wireframes (you know, with those squiggly lines that denote "content goes here"). Leaving interface design almost to the end may run counter to your user experience (UX) instincts. But for structured content, you really want to design structure first. You'll use that to connect content *resources* (for now, think of those as individual articles on specific topics, a bit like Wikipedia). Finally, you'll design all the ways you want those resources to be represented. Web pages. Mobile apps. Kiosk displays. That's where the wireframing comes in. (But hey, if you want to impress your stakeholders with a few early conceptual mock-ups, go right ahead! Even Walt Disney used artists' impressions to convince his backers long before breaking ground on his theme parks.)

You're probably onboard with the idea of a research and discovery phase. But the research we're interested in is about the subject domain itself. And the first people we'll get you to speak to aren't users, or even stakeholders, but subject-matter *experts* (SMEs). Hold on, that doesn't sound like good UX advice either! Don't panic—we're both from a UX background and wouldn't dream of telling you to skimp on researching general user needs. But our focus is on designing a connected content structure, and that means knowing your subject.

LITTLE THINGS MEAN A LOT

We believe you should design your content structure around real-world things. When people read a web page or watch a video or browse a photo gallery, what's interesting to them isn't that they're looking at a document, a photo, or a moving image. They're far more interested in the content of that media—what it's *about*. Inherent to any content you create are one or more specific examples of concepts. Bob Dylan. The Volkswagen Beetle. The three-olive martini. People don't care about the containers; they care about the *things* they contain.

Things in the real world have readily understood relationships to other things. The content (for example, a scene from the TV show *Mad Men*) puts these things in a particular context. But they can also act as gateways connecting us to whole other topics. From Dylan to folk music. From the Beetle to automobiles. From martinis to mixology. If you've spent time free-associating via Wikipedia links, you know how that goes.

You only understand something relative to something you already understand.

—Richard Saul Wurman

Even within a topic, linking content based on its real-world relationships helps everyone make sense of it. We all understand that the songwriter *writes* the song. That the scientist *performs* the experiment. Or that the giant panda *eats* shoots and leaves. And should it happen that someone doesn't know, the link between two concepts actually teaches them something new about how the world joins up.

Connecting the Natural World

Once upon a time lived a man named Tom. Tom was a product manager at the BBC in London. His vision was to build a natural history website that would inform, educate, and even entertain people as it taught them how the fauna and flora of the natural world are connected.

The BBC is one of the world's most well-respected broadcasters. Since 1922, they've consistently produced high-quality radio and television shows, including many hours of award-winning natural history documentaries. But when it comes to digital strategy, it's fair to say their approaches weren't always successful. This large and fragmented corporation wasn't immune to siloed thinking. Small web teams, working in different parts of the business, spent time and money on hand-crafted throwaway microsites. Sites that launched with fanfare, when the show they supported was on the air, were left to wither once that show was forgotten. Digital education teams created perfectly good guides to Henry VIII and Winston Churchill, seemingly unaware of the similar resources published by the History team two years previously. Yet more teams were doing their best with a shoestring budget to produce text articles on the solar system or pregnancy, despite high-budget video content already bought and paid for and sitting unused in the BBC television archives.

This last point intrigued Tom greatly. He could base his natural history product on something no other content provider had: 50 years of stunning BBC wildlife documentaries.

He started designing, not with an interface sketch or a wireframe, but with the work of the 18th-century Swedish botanist Carl Linnaeus. The Linnaean taxonomy arranges the natural world into domain, kingdom, phylum, class, order, family, genus, and species. It's really the go-to classification model for the animal kingdom. As information architectures go, this was a leg up. Tom took elements from this model and created his own simplified version, adding things, like habitats, adaptations, and conservation status, that wildlife enthusiasts had shown interest in.

Tom let this model guide him as he and his team researched the television archives looking for possible content. Having already spelled out the kinds of things he wanted to include, the mission now was simply to find small pieces of focused content about individual animals, habitats, environments, and behaviors.

The BBC content yielded many treasures, but Tom wasn't finished. He also needed a text description for each animal. The description would be featured on a page dedicated solely to that animal. For this he turned to Wikipedia, where content is liberally licensed for reuse. Some Wikipedia articles weren't all that great, so Tom's team improved that content— directly on Wikipedia so that everyone could benefit. Likewise, he pulled in conservation status data from the University of Michigan's Museum of Zoology, who make it freely available on their Quaardvark tool.

Tom's Wildlife Finder product was a hit. It remixed BBC content with other authoritative sources in new and useful ways, connected by navigation that showed how the natural world joins up. As one of the first BBC products designed in this way, it also showed the corporation a new way of approaching digital content—weaving together a single, extensible network of knowledge.

IT'S DESIGN ALL THE WAY DOWN

As we write this, debate rages on Twitter (when doesn't it?) about what it means to "design" something. Opinions are split on whether it's fair to say that everyone on a product team is a designer or whether that, um, designation should be reserved for those who come to work with sharp haircuts and their top button fastened, ready to push pixels. The concern seems to be that if everyone is a designer, is no one a designer? And does this open the floodgates for the sales manager to weigh in on what color she thinks the app icon should be?

We daresay such fears stem from a limited notion of design. Digital product design isn't just the layout, styling, and decoration of the things you can see. Of course, interfaces are hugely important and absolutely require expert care and attention to make sure they're useful and usable (to say nothing of delightful, distinctive, and de-lovely). But design doesn't stop at the surface. User interfaces connect people to the business and, more immediately, to the business's content.

Getting the content structure right is design. Designing the content itself is design. After all, the content is the whole damn point. It's why people are coming to your product in the first place. But if you start design with interface wireframes, a lot of things get lumped together. Decisions about structure, layout, hierarchy, navigation, and even editorial priority can rest on the shoulders of the interface designer.

By focusing first on structure, then on content design, and finally on interfaces, you separate these concerns. Your cross-functional project team members can each bring their superpowers to bear, and everyone gets to do what they do best. When you do get to interface design, you'll find decisions far easier to make. As a team, you'll have a clear idea of how the subject domain would best be represented. Designing from the content out, rather than the interface in, helps ensure that the visual presentation shows off the content at its best. A lot of your navigation decisions will be taken care of by the connections defined in your structure. You'll be using content itself as a design material to craft the best experience for every device. Think of structured content as the design behind the design.

> *Design is putting form and content together.*
>
> *—Paul Rand*

TEAMWORK MAKES THE DREAM WORK

Design is political. Designing a subject domain, doubly so. You're codifying a point of view on what a subject is. That goes deep, starting tremors that reverberate through an entire product. Keeping a design project on the rails is a contact sport. It takes influence and persuasion. Clarifying the roles and responsibilities. Getting a high-level commitment to safeguard the things we hold dear.

Designing structure first flushes out complexity early. Puts on the table the things most likely to cause disagreement. When you lay down the first draft of your model, you can be sure of some healthy debate. Get the team and stakeholders aligned on the world you want to represent and you'll set up the rest of the project for success. Unlike wireframes, models let your team evaluate structure alone. They're conceptual, which helps project sponsors feel comfortable in lending their business expertise. And they're technical, which helps engineers understand early the kind of system they'll be expected to create and contribute to.

Considering structure helps everyone on the team find a level of altitude where they all basically agree. It's a common ground where everyone can offer valid feedback. Disagreements may come further down the line as you get into content and interface design. But at least you know there's a place where you're all facing the same way. Agree on the strategy; argue the tactics.

BECOMING FUTURE FRIENDLY

Not every benefit of adopting structured content will be felt right away. In the short term, you'll build an efficient, richly linked ecosystem that helps users find what they're looking for and helps your content creators focus on what they do best. You'll be shaping your content into small, sharable, reusable pieces to get the most use out of them. You'll have a clear strategy for which content is most useful to invest in.

But that's just for right now. You're also setting yourself up for future success. When structured around real-world concepts and connections, content scales up without breaking (just look at Wikipedia's 40 million articles for proof of that). When you separate content and structure from presentation, you're in great shape to design interface representations for any new device that comes along. And when that content is described with metadata, right down to the last attribute, then every new device—even those without screens—can offer a completely tailored experience based on the same content. Chatbot? Sure. VoiceUI skill? Why not. Heck, people don't even have to come through your digital front door to get at your content. Do a Google search for movie show times in your area. You'll get the information you need without ever leaving the search results. That's not the future; that's today.

Of course success depends on having good content. The most intricate structure in the world isn't a lot of use if you're publishing stuff that no one needs. Later in this book, we'll share some thoughts about what "good" content means. Researching your audience's mental model of the subject domain is a great way to start. The domain model you'll construct maps a territory perhaps larger than the content you can supply today. But that model will still be valid tomorrow, when your content budget is bigger. And chances are it'll remain so in three-ish years when your board decides it's time for a website makeover.

We call it thinking "future friendly." Preparing your content for whatever new devices and modes of consumption may come along. Finding new ways to share your content with people, wherever they are. Building new windows on your world.

CHAPTER BY CHAPTER

Before we get started, let's run through what each chapter will cover. While the linear nature of books suggests a production-line process, the truth is that you'll revisit each major step regularly. Your research informs your modeling, but your modeling can uncover unanswered questions that need more research. Your content design stems from a well-defined content model, but digging into examples of content can quickly uncover all those gnarly exceptions you forgot to account for. As with most projects, there are a lot of plates to keep spinning. Jump around these chapters as you need to.

In Chapter 2, we look at the changing digital landscape. The last ten years have seen an explosion of devices—most notably, the rise of mobile as the dominant platform for consuming digital content. In turn, we've all changed our habits in how we find that content through search and social media and how we share it with our friends. To address these behavioral shifts, businesses like yours need to improve how they commission and maintain digital projects. To avoid lapsing into triennial cycles of redesign, a business has an opportunity to set itself up for future success by separating its interface designs from the underlying content structure. By investing steadily in ongoing content management and governance, they'll make sure the right content reaches the right audience. Respect the role of digital content in driving business success. "The website" is no longer a one-off item way down on the meeting agenda and dismissed as an "IT problem." If you're in the business of attracting an audience and growing your customer base, then digital publishing and communication is core business.

Chapter 3 dives into what we mean by "structured content." Spoiler alert: it's content that gets broken into small parts so that those parts can be recombined one way on a desktop web page, another way in a mobile app, and a third way when, say, heard through a voice interface like Amazon's Alexa. For that magic to work properly, you feed the computer some rules about how different kinds of content relate. You tell it that if you're publishing something about an engineering landmark (such as the Golden Gate Bridge), then that piece will include details like its location, year of completion, and claim to fame. And when you later design a page in your website or app for a landmark, you can make room for those descriptive properties, knowing that the computer has the information it needs to fill them out with specific content. Page designs come and go. Devices and platforms may rise and fall. But the structural integrity of your content can stand firm, making every redesign easier. Designing with structure is a gift to your future self.

In Chapter 4 you'll start to get hands-on with designing connected content. That begins with researching your subject domain with the help of SMEs, audience representatives, and your own Google-fu. You'll sniff out the most important concepts in the domain and understand how they connect. You'll learn which stuff is most important to your core audience and where their terminology or mental model differs from the expert view. You'll come away able to bluff your way through the subject pretty well, able to help your team understand the world you're all designing for.

Chapter 5 takes this research and funnels it into the construction of a domain model. It's a diagram that communicates all you've learned about how the key concepts within your subject domain hang together. It acts as a shared reference point for your team and quickly flushes out any misunderstandings or disagreements before getting into engineering, where changes are expensive. The domain model becomes your astronomical chart of the content universe. This is the territory you'll fill out with content, one piece at a time.

In Chapter 6, you'll add more detail as the high-level domain model turns into a more focused content model. This is where you describe each of those key concepts through their constituent properties and plan out the various types of content that you'll eventually bring to the screen. By the end of this, you'll have a detailed plan for your content's structure.

We look at content itself in Chapter 7. This isn't a book about how to write copy or shoot video, but we offer some principles for well-designed content that meets user needs. You'll use the work you've done in content modeling to chop up content into small pieces that the computer connects together based on the relationships you defined. This is where we talk about blobs and chunks—neither sounds pleasant, but they'll help you understand the difference between unstructured "dumb" content and super-intelligent structured content.

Chapter 8 covers the back end of content management. You'll take all your research, modeling, and content design and make it all work for your content management system (CMS). We'll talk about CMSs in general, why you shouldn't feel bad for hating yours, and things to consider when shopping for one. Many businesses working with structured content actually develop their own CMS, or at least heavily customize an existing one. But it's perfectly possible to have a great structured solution with an off-the-shelf product, provided you make the right choices. Planning for CMS implementation adds yet more detail to your content model, spelling out field by field the interface an author will use to enter content according to your designed structure.

In Chapter 9, we help you bring all that content glamour to the big screen. Or the small screen. Maybe even the chatbot. We'll look at how interfaces are designed for structured content. Each interface is like a window on the world. Peering through that glass, you experience the vista of content that stretches out on the other side. We'll look at how each interface can remix different chunks of content. We'll explore navigation options and how they can come from your original domain model. And we'll discuss (for what by then will probably be the millionth time) how separating interface design from content design makes redesign projects so much less painful.

Finally, in Chapter 10 we look to the future, because that's how people normally end a book like this. For some businesses, the internet is still space age. Even today they drag themselves into cyberspace with an enthusiasm reserved for a root canal. But "new media" isn't new anymore, and the tectonic plates of the digital landscape are forever restless. So this is where we'll help you convince your boss that by investing in structure they'll get better digital products that improve return on investment, make the most of content already paid for, and better prepare for a future where the means of finding, consuming, and sharing content look nothing like they do today.

CLIMBING THE SUMMIT

As we progress, we'll keep coming back to a real project we worked on a few years ago: a conference on the topic of information architecture (IA). The Association for Information Science & Technology (ASIS&T) has hosted the IA Summit event every year since its inception in 2000. Over the years, minds immeasurably superior to ours have shared their IA expertise through talks, slides, workshops, and more. It was some of these folks who taught us about content management. Yet sadly, the IA Summit's own website struggled to practice what the event preached. Year after year, a site would be built for the upcoming conference. The site detailed all the speakers and their sessions, along with information about the venue and local area. The designers even went to the trouble of making a schedule timetable page, which worked pretty great until we all started using our phones to browse the web. And when the conference was done for the year, the whole thing was torn down, never to be used again.

We thought there was a better way. Our goal was to build something not just for the next conference, but for every IA Summit thereafter. Not only would this break the cycle of redesign, but it could become an increasingly valuable asset. The event aims to be the home of conversation about the craft of information architecture. It has a community of ardent fans who come first as attendees but often return as speakers or workshop hosts. Some go on to help out with the programming and production of the conferences themselves.

> *Always design a thing by considering it in its next larger context. A chair in a room, a room in a house, a house in an environment, an environment in a city plan.*
>
> —*Eliel Saarinen*

With a multi-event structure, we could track each participant's contributions and roles over time. We could cross-reference topics discussed at the latest event with related thinking from five years back. We could use the pages created to advertise each session and to host the slides and recordings for the session after the fact. We could use the structure to house a growing knowledge repository for the benefit of the wider community. When you're doing the information architecture for a conference about information architecture, you really want to get it right.

That ambition led us to design our structure based on things common to every event—to the overall subject domain of the IA Summit (maybe even to conferences in general). Things like sessions, people, venues, sponsors, topics, and tracks. We would go on to find content for every example of these things and use the relationships between them to connect that content. As we learned more about the domain, we discovered that some things didn't join up exactly as we assumed they did. And we found that other things become a bit complicated when you're thinking about more than one event.

It's a pretty good example with which to chart the progression from research to structural design to content planning and publishing. We'll take you down the path we followed, including a few wrong turns.

Designing connected content goes from the bottom up. You first aim for stability by considering a subject domain. From there you look at the structure of content and the makeup of that content itself. Finally you consider how to represent the content resources, since interface design is perhaps the most rapidly changing part of all. Yet all these elements must be kept in balance for a truly successful product. Design each part with its surroundings in mind.

In the end, it's all about making connections. Along the way you'll connect with the people in your organization so that your product may benefit from their expertise. You'll connect to your audience to learn about the things that matter to them. And you'll forge new bonds between the elements of your content itself, expressing relationships to build understanding. It's connection that makes the elements more valuable than the sum of their parts.

CHAPTER 2

WHY WE NEED A NEW WAY OF APPROACHING DIGITAL CONTENT

Organizations are creating more content than ever. Endless website redesigns, excessive numbers of microsites to manage, and siloed content marketing channels all contribute to a plethora of content. Keeping up with new interfaces where your content needs to display seems like a losing race. It doesn't have to be this way. Take a step back and take a deep breath to get a grip on your content. There is another way that is better for your organization and better for your audience.

DOES THIS SOUND FAMILIAR?

You've launched a new website that took months (or years) to create. You're excited about it, and you tell your audience (and board) all about it. It is gorgeous to look at, easy to use, and completely responsive. You ride the excitement for a few months. But the newness wears off. More and more pages get added by people putting their content wherever they think is a good place on the site. Everyone's attention has moved on to the next shiny object. The website starts to fall into disrepair.

This goes on for another year, and people start to complain that they can't find anything on the website anymore. Design trends have changed, and the site no longer looks "modern." You stop referring people to the website because you're embarrassed about it.

It seems the only thing to do is do a full redesign—rework the navigation, structure, content, design, *and* content management system (CMS). Because the website is important, it gets a substantial budget, and the project is high priority. And so the cycle starts again (**FIGURE 2.1**).

FIGURE 2.1 Product neglect leads to an increasingly negative experience, eventually requiring an expensive redesign.

Slow decline leading to "we need a new website!"

Iterative improvement based on structured content

 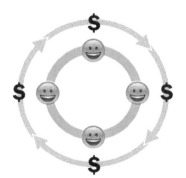

Or maybe you recognize this pattern: Your organization is launching an initiative next month. The default reaction is "we need a microsite." That's what was done with other campaigns and initiatives, and it needs to be ready fast. You don't have time to see how it fits with the other sites you've already got, because they are such a tangled mess. What's one more site among the 10, 50, or 100+ you already have?

The problem isn't just too much content on too many websites. Each marketing channel has its own content created for it. Often there is no real connection between an organization's product, website, blog, Facebook page, and YouTube channel, or all the other places content gets published. The people creating the content for one channel may have little communication with the content creators for the other channels. Instead of complementing each other by driving toward the same goal, internal groups end up competing for attention and resources.

These patterns are unsustainable. They are expensive, disruptive, and inefficient. They focus on short-term solutions to solve immediate problems rather than on a strategy for long-term success. Over time, the result is a tangled mess of digital properties and content that gets reorganized, rewritten, redesigned, and moved into a new CMS at great cost. Repeatedly and regularly.

TAKE A STEP BACK

It's time to rethink our approach to creating and publishing content to maximize investment, make experiences coherent across devices and platforms, and ensure we meet audience needs efficiently and effectively.

The future is uncertain. New technologies, new devices, and new interfaces will always affect where content shows up and how people interact with and use it. What we do know is that the future will include screenless interfaces and algorithms to interpret our needs and connect us to the information we seek.

The solution to all this is to start thinking about content in a broader context, outside of an interface. We need to design content that is stored, structured, and connected outside any user interface, in a way that's readable and understandable by both people and computers.

This deliberate, forward-looking way of planning and creating content solves many of the problems organizations face in the third decade of the worldwide web. It benefits the business and its customers, the people working on the content, design teams, stakeholders, and the web as a whole.

A NEW APPROACH

Let's look at how designing content that is future-friendly and connecting it across multiple channels provides a better long-term return on investment.

BETTER FOR BUSINESS

In their budgets for marketing and technology, organizations spend massive amounts of money to maintain an online presence and keep customers or members or donors coming in the door. Digital products need to show measurable value. By thinking about how to better invest in digital content now, you'll be in a better position in the long run.

MAKE CONTENT WORK HARDER

Although much fuss is made about what a website looks like and which content management system to use, content—not the design or technology—is the whole point of what businesses do. The point of websites is for people to access information or complete a task. We need to make sure we're creating something of value. Each piece of content we create needs to match to a defined user need and business objective to give it meaning and provide a way to measure value.

A piece of content can appear in many places. It is hardly ever viewed only on a single web page and nowhere else. Consider all the places on the website, as well as on other systems, that it could be displayed. Never assume that a piece of content will have only one destination. Rather than re-creating content for each channel, create it once and publish it everywhere.

Before creating something new, look at what is already in your inventory and pull it together in a new way. Think of yourself as a curator. Don't re-create things that already exist. When you break content into its smallest pieces, you can mix and match it in many ways—much like an art museum. One year it has an exhibit of paintings by 19th-century French artists. Another year it has one of impressionists. Each one uses a subset of Claude Monet paintings, perhaps with different exhibit cards highlighting different qualities of the paintings. Even though the exhibits are made from familiar elements, the curators have told a new story through the threads they chose to weave together in the new curation. They would not re-create the paintings because there was a different context.

Museums can tell many stories with the same artifacts by reorganizing them, creating new displays, and curating the objects in different ways. Planning ahead and structuring your content saves you from having to re-create similar content and lets you put together new interfaces faster to tell a new story. Is your content working hard for you?

HELP PEOPLE FIND YOUR CONTENT

People need to find your content for it to be useful to them. In a world of billions of web pages, people rely on search engines to get them to where they want to go. Therefore, your content needs to show up near the top of search engine results for relevant terms. It's a competitive world, and it takes more than keyword research to make it to the top of the results.

Give search engines what they want: entities. Around the internet, within your own website, and among your properties, you should have a single content resource per thing, no matter how many ways it is chunked up and displayed. All that almost-the-same-but-separate content written by different teams within the same company confuses search engines and the people trying to figure out which link to click. You need an organization-wide plan for publishing. That plan needs to include creating content that your audience cares about and using technology and content structure in a way that allows Google's webcrawlers to easily find and display it.

BE READY FOR NEW TECHNOLOGY

So many devices and screen sizes and viewports exist that it is impossible to account for all the ones that are available today, let alone the ones that will be in our pockets in three years. When we create a website or product, we have no idea what a visitor will use to access it, where they'll be, or what their connection speed will be. We need to plan for this infinite combination of sizes and uses. And that means making content machine-readable, ready for any artificial intelligence to repurpose and deliver in multiple ways.

If content is tied to design and visual cues that rely on human inference to interpret meaning, there is no way for it to be ready for voice recognition tools, smart homes, or wearables. Just because we can't imagine something doesn't mean we shouldn't be prepared to meet sudden demand. There was a time when we couldn't access the internet on a phone. Many businesses didn't believe that there would be a need for people to get *their* content on such a small screen. Turns out, they were quite wrong. Don't be left behind just because you can't imagine a use case for your content to be found by a person five years from now on a device you can't fathom today. Plan your content for time travel by making it accessible to algorithms and portable from one system to another.

MAKE REDESIGNS ABOUT VISUAL DESIGN

Even though it's not the most important thing, it does matter how visually appealing a website is. Design trends change, and it can be easy for your site to look outdated, even if your content is excellent. With the right structure for your content, you can keep up with what looks modern without reconstructing the entire thing.

Too often, "redesign" means tearing down the entire site and rebuilding it, including the navigation structure, content, and CMS. If you get the structure and content right from the start, then changing the look is truly cosmetic—only the look changes. Like putting new slipcovers on a sofa, getting some new pillows, and painting the walls a new color. Much easier, faster, and less expensive than tearing up the floors, throwing out the old furniture, and moving the walls. You might want to change the design every few years, but do it as a refresh of visual design, not because the site has become unusable. With a plan for content to remain meaningful across interfaces and available for restyling, website redesigns become more a visual exercise than a giant project.

INCREASE RETURN ON INVESTMENT

Are you getting the idea that all this extra content is expensive? It is! Digital products need to pay their own way, delivering on business and customer needs. Those who control the purse strings are starting to expect a return on the investment.

The continuous cycle of spending five, six, or even seven figures regularly on new websites that don't deliver results is a drag on the bottom line. If you aren't already, soon you may be required to justify expense and show how you're contributing to revenue. If you are responsible or accountable for the website's strategic performance, expect to provide proof of success. Planning content with an eye on reuse and longevity will help keep costs down while helping improve revenue streams.

BETTER FOR TEAMS

Getting all the people involved in producing websites and digital products on the same page can be the most difficult part of any project. We are not promising magic, but a benefit of keeping the focus on content over interfaces is easier alignment among and between teams as well as between the organization and its audiences.

DESIGN TEAM

A certain level of disagreement on priorities or emphasis may exist among the design team—or web team or UX team or marketing team, whatever yours is called. Leadership, priorities, and overall project direction are often determined by seniority, the loudest voice, or sheer numbers (for example, one content strategist for every eight to ten designers and developers). Cross-functional teams with balanced representation tend to find more efficient ways of collaborating, where everyone's contribution is valued and no effort is wasted. Beginning design outside the interface naturally enhances collaboration. It is a great equalizer because the focus is on the big picture rather than on each person's role. The emphasis is on the input and outcome and finding the best way between those two points.

STAKEHOLDERS

With your design team aligned, you can get the benefit of stakeholder expertise and input when it matters most: before designing, building, or writing anything. Having stakeholders involved early and often will lower the chances of last-minute changes based on a high-level person's opinion. As you'll see as you go through this book, the process of starting with research and moving through modeling and implementation provides many stakeholder check-in points.

Research activities create space for stakeholders to share their knowledge and instruct the design team about what the concepts are and how they fit together. When you aren't talking about web designs or navigation menus, you are gathering information rather than opinion-based web design. Getting small pieces of input and showing concepts throughout the project reduces the effect of politics and streamlines the process.

AUDIENCE

Many organizations still design and create content based on what they *think* their audience wants, not on what the audience *actually* wants. A website needs to be useful *and* usable. (Though your site might be perfectly usable, your audience may not want any of the things on it.) It is important to get the internal team and stakeholders focused on the right audience and what they want, as well as on what vocabulary the audience uses.

Use input from user research to help stakeholders see the overlap between their world and the audience's. The result is a persistent mental model that guides future content development, which in turn shapes what interfaces to create (rather than the idea of an interface dictating what content gets created).

Usability vs. Usefulness

Funny things happen when you do usability testing and listen to what participants say about the content, not just about the functionality. One time, Carrie's team was testing whether the forms for a new webinar subscription service were usable. They knew they had to make sure users weren't frustrated when the service launched. The good news: All the participants found it easy to complete the signup.

However, the comments of several of the participants were concerning. They said that although they completed the signup during the test, they would not necessarily have done so with their own money. Whoa! "Tell us more."

Turns out that they had unanswered questions, such as "How long do I have to use this?" and "Can I split this with a colleague?" Without understanding the full terms of the subscription, they were not likely to spend $500. And they were not likely to ask the questions; they would just pass on the offer. A usable interface for a service people didn't want to buy isn't very useful.

With just a few changes to the content, both on the website and in the marketing material, the questions were answered, and the campaign launched with more confidence that the conversion goals would be met.

COLLABORATION ACROSS GROUPS

Within most organizations, silos are strong. People are doing different things with different priorities. That includes both silos between various departments and silos within design teams. The best outcomes happen when everyone focuses on the same things and has the same priorities. Instead of dividing attention across functions, different groups need to work together toward the same outcome. Content is an output of most groups. Shouldn't it be coordinated?

By starting with the question "What is going to be on the website?" we end up with a very tactical and emotional discussion. Everyone fights for their piece of the limited space on the home page and for a top-level menu slot. In these discussions, the squeaky wheel usually wins.

When you start by defining the domain in which your business operates—answering "Where do we fit in the bigger world?"—you help your organization beyond getting better content. It helps with the politics within the organization itself. Because you are elevating the conversation to be about what your stakeholders care most about—their area of expertise—you are more likely to avoid arguments about what goes on the home page.

Once you get that alignment, you can start to prioritize. Within every discipline or company, there are some basic facts or principles that need to be followed. If you can base your website's prioritization on real-world priorities rather than perceived screen real estate value, you'll be much better off. The time you take to get the buy-in for the *what* before the *how* will be more than made up for later.

MAKE IMPROVEMENTS FASTER

By separating the layers with greater persistence from those that are subject to change, you can deliver improvements and respond to customer needs faster. By creating content in smaller, modular pieces that are used across all interfaces, we can change exactly what needs to be changed instead of the whole thing.

Maybe you find that a particular call to action isn't working. After some A/B testing, you discover the right combination of design and text for a button on a website. Sitewide changes can be made with two small changes: updates in the CMS text field that holds that call-to-action text and the CSS that controls the button design. No searching through the whole site hoping you remember where all the instances of that call to action are. Incremental change is more palatable because it is easy and requires only the resources you already have. All these small improvements add up to better conversion rates and happier customers.

CONTRIBUTE TO THE WORLD WIDE WEB

Your website is a window on your world. Your content is part of the wider world, both offline and online. It's important to remember that your audience cares less about your brand than about getting things done or having a question answered. That means you need to think about where your content fits in that wider world, not just about a single interface.

Make the mental shift of thinking about web pages as sets of information displayed together rather than as a discrete thing. Create content so that it's free to go wherever it wants to go, not just on the website you have right now. Then you can start creating the web that Tim Berners-Lee dreamed of in the first place. In 2008, 20 years after he created the worldwide web, he encouraged modularity in the systems being built:

> We should always be looking to make a clean system with an interface ready to be used by a system which has not yet been invented . . . . Messy interfaces introduce complexity which we may later regret.
>
> —*Tim Berners-Lee, from "Simple Things Make Firm Foundations"* (*www.w3.org/blog/2008/01/modularity/*)

Let's create clean systems and get rid of the messiness by focusing on what we can do today to be ready for tomorrow.

How to Get Started with Domain Modeling

AN INTERVIEW WITH ANNETTE PRIEST

Annette Priest heads up Strategic UX & Product Design for health care at the Advisory Board, a research and best practices firm specializing in education and health care. As a leader in the user experience community, she helps companies solve problems in new and sometimes unexpected ways.

Tell me about the Advisory Board and your role.

The Advisory Board is a research and best practices firm. I work on health care technology products. We have a variety of products with varying levels of age and maturity across many platforms. We have a lot of information across the products and functional areas.

I lead an international team of researchers and designers. We serve all products based on their level of maturity and need. My team works directly with product management, development, and engineering, and tangentially with support and sales.

Do you act as an in-house design agency?

Yes. We were previously embedded in product teams and now have shifted toward a more in-house consultancy model.

Why did you undertake domain and content modeling?

I saw a strategic opportunity for the firm in terms of digital and product strategy and to help our own operations. For example, it could help our research division maximize the return on investment of their content by delivering it through various products and channels.

We are trying to get to a place of "create once, publish everywhere." Modeling gets us closer to that. Specifically for product development, it ensures that we reuse information in ways that are meaningful and valuable to the people who use our products and services.

Do you have a lot of duplicate content?

I don't know. My hope is that we can the find places where information is redundant once we have our models. We want content creators to have an easier and more meaningful way to begin their content creation—starting from what we already have. Even if the content is aging, modeling could be foundational for creating content more quickly and efficiently.

(continues)

(continued)

What challenges did you face to get this process approved?

It's complicated, but the short story is that the initial work overlapped with an initiative we were already undertaking. I was able to advance domain and content modeling as a way to move that work forward rather than as an investment in a new approach.

Our first project was a pilot to test the approach. Even if we did nothing else, it would help with that product. It was a baby-step approach: Spend a little money for the pilot and continue to scale and institute it more widely.

I needed to get executives from other functions to buy in to the concept so we could get time with their people, who we would interview as subject matter experts. In that sense, there is selling still to be done. It's important to understand how the other business divisions will benefit from modeling. It is up to me to translate how it is has tangible benefits for them.

Who have been the biggest champions outside of your team?

With each iteration we understand each other a little more. It requires effort to get to a shared understanding. Having a physical representation (in the form of models) of what's happening and who's involved and what action is taking place has been helpful. Knowing the benefit of domain modeling and tailoring that for people from different functions has helped. That requires time and effort and vision—lots of communication. Patience is essential. We have to be okay with participation being a sign of success.

What challenges do you foresee in getting this methodology more widely accepted throughout the company?

We need to help the research group see the benefit to their digital world. It's a challenge to help them understand how it affects their ability to find content and make it available to both internal users and customers. We need to make the case that modeling has an internal business value, which requires education.

What are some ways you plan to keep the interest and patience of other groups for this long-term work?

We need to help other groups identify needs that can be more immediately addressed. As a result of our conversations so far, there is a better appreciation of how this work makes content more findable.

How does domain modeling help the firm?

It addresses a few different pain points. One particular problem we've discovered is that people spend too much time tracking down content. That means staff are starting from scratch too often and aren't able to point customers to existing information.

They spend a lot of time training new employees. A domain model can help people get up to speed more quickly. Other teams can spend time coming to a shared understanding more quickly.

It allows people to work across functions within the company while preserving flexibility and independence. They can maintain their independent process but collaborate better.

As for our product strategy, modeling allows us to build better products with modern interfaces.

Do you expect it to lower the lifetime cost of your product?

From a pilot perspective, no. But at scale, yes. What's really valuable about this approach is getting people to draw the line on where something begins and ends and how it fits together with other things. You have puzzle pieces that fit together. When dealing with such a complex product space and portfolio, it's important to know where things begin and end. It's important to know what's tangential, peripheral, adjacent—and where innovation can happen.

Any other thoughts on how others can get started?

I can't overemphasize how important it is to start small. Have something well-defined and scoped and continue in that area. That way, work can grow organically. I couldn't do this all over the place. Biting off just the right amount to get the momentum going is all you need to do. Focus on your own backyard.

CHAPTER 3

UNDERSTANDING STRUCTURED CONTENT

Freedom, flexibility, and time travel are possible for your content if you give it structure. Breaking down content into small parts makes it more usable, useful, and accessible. Don't just make the right content, make content right.

SETTING CONTENT FREE

"Prose is architecture, not interior decoration."

—*Ernest Hemingway*

Content wants to be free. Like Lego. The bricks don't change, but they can be taken apart and put back together. Add and remove bricks and reconfigure them to form a vacation house, a police station, a ship, a tree, the Millennium Falcon.

Content wants to travel through time and from place to place. It wants to be useful today as part of a website displayed in Google Chrome on a laptop and tomorrow as a response from Amazon Echo's Alexa. And five years from now it will want to be useful as a heads-up display in a car or projected onto someone's arm from a wristband. It can all be the same content—if you set it up properly.

Though it sounds contrary, giving content structure means giving it more flexibility and freedom. This is because you are not tied to your first idea for delivery when you create it. By planning the structure before the content itself, you can decide later how to fill it up and put it together. You can put the same content together in different ways over and over again. Just like Lego.

Before we dive into figuring out what content to create, let's get clear on what structured content is and how it is essential to designing connected content.

WHAT IS STRUCTURED CONTENT?

Structured content is content that is planned, developed, and connected outside an interface so that it's ready for any interface. It allows you to define the skeleton of your content before you create it. Breaking content into the smallest pieces possible (within reason) so that it is free to go anywhere, anytime.

As you'll see in the modeling and designing chapters, structured content is based on concepts and resources and entities—not on web pages. This is because a web page is merely one way to deliver and display content. An app screen is another. And an Alexa skill is yet another way that content is delivered but not even displayed.

Start by considering the meaning and subject of content itself, rather than the ways in which it will be delivered. Prioritize your content resources before your interface representations. The content you create is a surrogate for something that exists outside the digital world you seek to create. An animal, a company, a country has defining characteristics that distinguish it from other examples of the same order. Structured content holds the characteristics of that thing so it can be represented in context by a website, an app, or a game. For each representation, the designer chooses which attributes to display and how they should appear.

Terms Related to Connected Content

Words matter. This is a book about content, after all. Let's define some terms we'll be using throughout this book. By understanding these terms, you'll gain entry into other worlds and be prepared for the future of content.

Attribute: A characteristic or inherent property of something; *synonym:* property

Concept: An idea that is inferred from specific instances; basis for content types and objects

Content: Substantive information that is expressed through a medium

Content type: A reusable container for storing content that has common structure and purpose

Domain: A sphere of knowledge, influence, or activity

Entity: A thing or concept that is unique, distinguishable, and self-contained

Instance: An example of a concept or object

Metadata: Machine-readable information that describes a thing

Model: A simplified visual representation of a system

Object: A variable or data structure that corresponds to something in the real world

Representation: Presentation of an idea or collection

Resource: A thing that can be identified and represented as a collection of parts

MOVING TOWARD STRUCTURED CONTENT

Structure has many meanings, even within the context of content and digital products. It is a way of organizing things. It is a way of building things. It is the arrangement of parts. And we want to organize, build, and arrange content to tell stories, provide helpful information at just the right time, and open different windows into the world in which we operate.

At the heart of it, structure comes from breaking content into reusable parts and defining the rules for how those parts should connect. We'll get into more depth about how to determine what those parts are for each type of content (Chapter 6) and how to build a system to support it (Chapter 8). But first, let's talk about how structure gives content flexibility and sets it up for wherever it needs to go.

GAINING FLEXIBILITY

A lot of web content still gets published as standalone "pages," created using a WYSIWYG (what you see is what you get) editor and held as an unstructured content blob in the body field of a design template. It has no inherent relationship with other pieces of content. Each blob stands alone unless manually linked together.

What we need are chunks. A chunk is a small, defined piece of content. It is pure content, devoid of any presentational styling. It's in a malleable form that can be reused over and over with any design and in any format.

Chunks set the content free. Words, images, videos, files, and widgets are all held separately, ready to be remixed and reconnected.

Metadata can be assigned to each chunk. That data about the data establishes specific meaning. Thus, the meaning is embedded in chunks so that computers can understand what it is, what it's about, and how it relates to other chunks. When all the chunks are put together, they provide a comprehensive understanding of a complete thing, or entity. The entity's metadata allows computers to read and understand the content in its constituent parts or as a whole.

The structure makes machine learning and artificial intelligence possible because the computers can connect content dynamically based on the cues humans give to it. That is way easier than managing every single web page and planning for all the possible combinations users might want.

BREAKING CONTENT INTO PARTS

Inherent structure is all around us. Look at your favorite music service. A song has a title, artist, genre, length, and year of release. A music store might add a rating and reviews. Identifying those constituent parts is the first step to organizing and arranging them.

Once you start down this road, you'll notice structure everywhere. Heck, we can no longer visit a website without thinking about how it is structured (or not). Begin by looking at the resource, the real-world thing, rather than at a single representation on the screen. What do music lovers most want to know about a song? What do attendees need to know about a conference session? What matters most to a journalist about a building?

Rather than talking in the abstract, let's walk through the process with some real content. Keep in mind that as we offer this example, we are making no judgment about the people who set this up originally. They are good people who did the best they could with the time, knowledge, and budget available at that time. Same as you, same as us.

EXISTING WEB PAGE OF UNSTRUCTURED CONTENT

FIGURE 3.1 shows an example of a web page about the Golden Gate Bridge that is unstructured and could use some help so that it can be reused in many contexts across the same website or even by other websites. After all, once the content is data with metadata attached, it can be turned into an application programming interface (API) or web service or otherwise scraped by crawlers that want to use the authoritative information about this thing. It becomes an entity.

If you looked at all 200 landmarks on the website, you'd notice the patterns and similar formatting across them all. Creating these required a human to remember and follow instructions to create consistency from one item to the next. Instead of resources, they were singular pages.

The index page that listed all the landmarks was also manually produced. When a new landmark was added, someone had to go to that page and figure out where in the list of landmarks it fit, put the cursor there, press Return, type the name of the landmark, and add a link to the landmark page.

FIGURE 3.1
A standard web page,
with no inherent
structure, about an
engineering landmark

Golden Gate Bridge, California

Home / Knowledge & Learning / People & Projects

Monument of the Millennium
Seven Modern Wonders of the World, 1994

One of the most recognized landmarks in the world, the Golden Gate Bridge, connects geographically isolated areas of California to the north, in Marin and Sonoma counties, with San Francisco. When the bridge opened in 1937, with a main suspension span length of 4,200 feet, it was the longest in the world. The engineering obstacles poised by the mile-wide, turbulent Golden Gate Strait led engineers to devise a bridge that required four years to build, 83,000 tons of steel, 389,000 cubic yards of concrete, and enough cable to encircle the earth three times. Previous ASCE designations for the Golden Gate Bridge include: the National Civil Engineering Landmark (1984) and Seven Wonders of the World (1955). Other significant bridges include the Verrazano-Narrows Bridge, the George Washington Bridge, the Akashi Kaikyo (Japan) and the Humber Bridge (England).

See the list of Seven Modern Wonders of the World.

Additional information

http://www.goldengatebridge.org/
The official web site for the Golden Gate Bridge, heralded as one of the top ten construction achievements of the 20th Century.

http://www.goldengatedesign.com/goldengate.html
Brief history of the massive construction project examines the politics, tragedies, and odds that seemed to hinder its completion.

http://www.thoma.com/thoma/ggbfacts.html
This fact sheet details the enormous Art Deco structure that details the bridge's design and lighting features.

http://www.goldengate.org/
Chronicles the planning and construction of the engineering marvel of the western world including several photographs.

ASCE presents these links for informational purposes only, without endorsement.

When you are the authoritative source for civil engineering in the United States, you want to show off feats of engineering and the engineers who created them. You want to make sure historic projects are highlighted wherever they are relevant. People, organizations, and websites all over the world want this information. By turning it into structured content (**FIGURE 3.2**), you can provide authoritative and credible content without having to do extra work when the content is desired elsewhere.

Engineering Project	Engineer
Project Name	First Name
Project Type	Last Name
Image	Suffix
Description	Credentials
Location	Birth Date
Claim to Fame	Death Date
Year Completed	Important Projects
Primary Engineer	Biography
	Photo

FIGURE 3.2
Engineering Project and Engineer content types hold all the content about a landmark and an engineer, respectively. Someone can pick and choose from the attributes to create a display.

Instead of redesigning the display, we created a content type for engineering projects generally. And we called it Engineering Project because the landmarks aren't all bridges or buildings and they aren't all historic. The Golden Gate Bridge is merely an instance of a project. While it helps to think of a few examples when deciding on the parts, don't be limited by those examples. Consider all the instances. Engineers are a separate entity because they have completely different attributes, and we may not want to display them with Engineering Projects.

All the parts do not have to be filled in for each instance. For example, some engineering projects have a noteworthy engineer associated with them, and others do not. Some have specific street addresses (U.S. Capitol), and others are located underground (first New York City subway).

See how having the content in pieces, rather than locked in one big mass creates freedom? Like Lego bricks, the pieces can be mixed and matched to provide just the right amount of detail for each instance. Oh, and if you want to change the data within this container, you need to change it in only one place and it's updated everywhere. Need a new field? Add it to the content type container, and every instance gets the attribute. Add a new item, and it's added wherever you've specified that content type to appear. Delete an instance, and it's removed everywhere it appeared.

USING STRUCTURED CONTENT

Breaking content down into parts sets you up to create different representations based on use case and context. Create the structure by thinking of all the ways you want to display the resource. Use the parts for specific representations.

ARRANGING

Arranging each instance individually would be a lot of work. And that is what you'd have to do if you have one web page for each of those 200 projects. Even starting with an example and duplicating it 199 times presents a time and energy challenge. You would have to create each page, assign a URL, and make sure the HTML code for the page name, body paragraphs, headings, images, and links are correct and properly placed so that it will display properly. Making links to other pages? Highlight the right text and then go to the other page to copy the URL and paste it into the WYSIWYG editor's box. Sure, the person creating the page is free to make choices about design, but are they qualified for that? This takes a lot of time, and human error is bound to creep in fast.

A structured content framework saves time and creates efficiencies. You arrange attributes in a template. You decide which attributes to show for a specific display, and design a display pattern that gets populated by the computer for each instance. When each project is displayed consistently and automatically, there is less room for human error.

For the Golden Gate Bridge, you might create three different templates that use various parts. The templates can have different styles applied to them. Each one uses only the attributes needed to convey a certain meaning or fulfill a user need. You might even want to bring in parts from different types of content (**FIGURES 3.3, 3.4,** and **3.5**).

Many considerations come into play when deciding what content to display and how to display it. We'll get to that in later chapters. Now you'll know what we're talking about when we get there (if you didn't already).

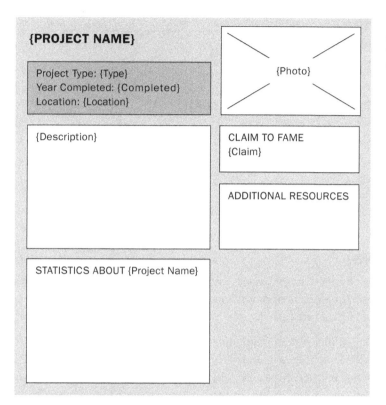

{PROJECT NAME}

Project Type: {Type}
Year Completed: {Completed}
Location: {Location}

{Photo}

{Description}

CLAIM TO FAME
{Claim}

ADDITIONAL RESOURCES

STATISTICS ABOUT {Project Name}

FIGURE 3.3 A template for the detailed display of a project using the `Engineering Project` content type.

CIVIL ENGINEERING LANDMARKS

More than 200 projects worldwide have earned the Historical Civil Engineering Landmark. Under challenging conditions, each of these engineering feats represents the achievement of what was considered an impossible dream.

PROJECT NAME ▼	TYPE ▼	LOCATION ▼	YEAR COMPLETED ▼
{Project Name}	{Project Type}	{Location}	{Completed}

FIGURE 3.4 Only the Project Name, Project Type, Location, and Year Completed fields for an `Engineering Project` are displayed in this template for a listing of projects.

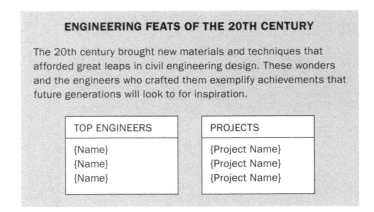

ENGINEERING FEATS OF THE 20TH CENTURY

The 20th century brought new materials and techniques that afforded great leaps in civil engineering design. These wonders and the engineers who crafted them exemplify achievements that future generations will look to for inspiration.

TOP ENGINEERS	PROJECTS
{Name}	{Project Name}
{Name}	{Project Name}
{Name}	{Project Name}

ORGANIZING

Once content is chunked up into pieces and arranged in various ways, it needs to be connected. The website or product needs to come together as a whole. That whole needs structure too.

The organization of the content might manifest itself as a sitemap or navigation structure. Or it might be a model of the world we are working within. Each type of content has relationships with other types. An Engineering Project is planned by an Engineer. An Engineer also connects to a Conference by being a Speaker. When you zoom out from the individual connections, you see a system that is complex but orderly—just like the things they are representing, whether that is civil engineering or your organization or the IA Summit community.

Whether you are breaking down content, arranging it on a page, or organizing a system, base the structure on real-world characteristics and relationships. You don't need to re-create things that already exist. The resources are already there; they just need new representations in a digital space.

WRITING CONTENT IS DIFFERENT TOO

Authoring is different when you structure your content. The default mode for most people who create content is to think their immediate publishing needs. Adding structure to content and creating resources instead of pages requires a new approach and mindset. You might meet resistance from your authors if you tell them to fill in a bunch of fields in which they cannot change the font or color. (On the other hand, some people will be delighted to have such clear guidelines. You can't make everyone happy!)

You can't just plop down a new content management system in front of your content authors, most of whom may not be writers in the first place. Everyone must be educated to understand this new way of creating content. As with the rest of this process, a bit of change management needs to happen. Collaborate, communicate, and educate to gain buy-in and give your content creators a sense of ownership.

You will need to create a content production process and educate authors about how they are part of a bigger world. Just as it is no longer sustainable to have a bunch of websites with blobs of content on them, it is not feasible to create content as if it has only one purpose. Train authors about how to create content in chunks so that it makes sense in all its representations. Show them how they fit into the bigger picture and how structured content behaves so they have proper context for creating it.

STRUCTURE EVERYWHERE

What about those pages that are not a concrete thing like an event, a person, a song, or a service? Even something that doesn't correspond to an entity—like your privacy policy or your terms and conditions—is still a resource. It has a URL, but it is singular and doesn't warrant its own content type. You could create an entity called `Basic Page` or `Article` that retains the flexibility of a big body field for times when there just isn't much structure or there's a unique type of content.

Entities with little inherent structure do exist, but they are few and far between. And they still need to be viewed and read and accessed by different screen sizes, in different browsers, and by people with differing abilities. Content must be structured in a way that still makes sense when recomposed for a small screen or read by a screen reader. That might have more to do with the underlying code than anything else, so be sure to work with your designers and engineers to make sure the content is represented accurately. Create as many separate fields as possible—even in your basic page. Those fields may need to travel too.

GO FORTH AND CREATE STRUCTURE

So far, we've outlined a process that makes your content better, longer lasting, and usable everywhere. To be successful, you need to shift your thinking from "What pages go on my website?" to "How do I structure the content about the world I'm representing with my digital product?"

You could conceivably chunk every bit and byte of content into the smallest particles that humans could imagine. The computer overlords would love it. But we live in the real world, where everything is imperfect and computers haven't quite taken over yet. To help them along, we need to create content with structure and purpose to be ready for machine learning and algorithmic processing. Don't think it won't happen to your content. Expect it and anticipate it.

Structured content is a lens into content strategy. Applying structure up front helps you get the right information to the right people at the right time—without re-creating it time and again. This is the basis of content strategy, which advocates a content-first approach to projects. Not just writing the right content, but creating it the right way to be useful and usable.

NOTE We do not talk specifically about DITA (Darwin Information Typing Architecture) or XML (Extensible Markup Language) or metadata strategies in this book. As with so many other things, there are whole books about them, and we encourage you to read them if you want to know more about the technical aspects of structured content. Here are two we recommend: *Metadata Basics for Web Content*, by Michael Andrews, and *Every Page Is Page One*, by Mark Baker. Our goal is to help you understand the basics so that you can be more prepared for the future.

STRUCTURING CONTENT

CHAPTER 4

RESEARCHING THE SUBJECT DOMAIN

Over the next few chapters, we'll go deep into our process for designing connected content. You'll plan out a foundational structure before filling that structure with content. That structure comes from the concepts and connections inherent to your content's subject matter. Your first mission is therefore one of discovery—researching your topic to tease out its main concepts and ideas, learning which areas appeal most to the people you design for, and capturing the terminology and language used to give form to the subject itself.

WHERE DO WE BEGIN?

Design begins with language—first, an understanding of the problem space shared with your project team, communicating your vision, and debating your differences until you reach alignment. And eventually, a solution that identifies and articulates some core concepts and the connections between them. Intuitive designs put into context the understanding we already have and extend our understanding to learn something new.

Let's say you're designing an app to help people choose a mortgage. You'd want them to understand fixed and variable interest, repayment periods, and mortgage types. You'd design navigation choices based on how these things relate in the world of mortgages. Your app would let people play around with different mortgage choices and learn how they differ from each other.

But chances are that as a designer or content specialist, you're not a mortgage expert, so you need to begin your research by leaning on the subject expertise of others.

DECONSTRUCTING SUBJECTS

Maybe you have mortgage amortization charts, a 10,000-page website on the history of art, or a smartwatch app that tracks your run. Your "content" might be as rich as long-form articles and expensive-looking videos or as simple as button labels or headings in an interface. But content is always *about* something. That something is a subject. A specialism or field of interest. Something researchable, like accountancy or organic food. Running. Fishing. Collecting retro video game consoles. Through content and code, your product and content strategy supports a *subject domain*.

That domain has structure. It has key concepts and relationships. For example, exploring art means studying artists, movements, styles, media, and, of course, the artworks themselves. Artists influence other artists, or sometimes an entire movement. They may work in paint or clay or marble, or any other medium. Artworks may hang in museums, galleries, or private collections around the world. Having interest in art means having interest in the things in that domain. To understand art is to understand how those things connect (**FIGURE 4.1**).

FIGURE 4.1
Rodin's *The Thinker* contemplating a mental model of the subject of art.

We made a case in previous chapters for using structured content in your digital projects—that is, to consider how pieces of content should hang together outside a user interface. All the interfaces built later represent some or all of that inherent content structure. How then do we go about designing the structure itself?

We begin our design process by studying and mapping the subject domain. Making cool smartphone and voice-controlled interfaces is great, but what's guiding your design decisions? Our premise is simple: Design your content and interfaces around the things people care about and you'll better serve those people's needs. There's a network of concepts and relationships inherent in any subject domain. Together, these provide an infrastructure to underpin all current and future work. It is the design behind the design.

WHAT'S MY DOMAIN?

What's your content about? We've worked on all kinds of projects, from a catalog for a paper manufacturer to a website for a civil engineering society. And always, there was an underlying subject of interest. People who buy paper in bulk want to know grade, grammage, weight, coating, and environmental certificates. This stuff doesn't just grow on trees, you know.

So, design content around that underlying subject. People's needs and interests don't begin and end with your business. They lie somewhere in the broader subject domain. People use Zillow and Rightmove because they're interested in real estate. They visit IMDb when they're curious about movie trivia. Think about your favorite apps and websites. What underlying subject domain do they serve?

- Airbnb—Travel
- Spotify—Music
- Instagram—Photography
- REI—The outdoors
- Shopify— Retail

Understanding the subject domain helps you develop a structure that supports your content. If people's interests really are rooted in that broader subject area, then it pays to use their mental model to connect your content together.

Through research, you'll figure out what your domain looks like and where its boundaries lie. It could be that it's incredibly broad, like "world history" or "marine biology." More likely, though, it's a little more focused—say, "World War II" or "tropical fish." As you get deeper into your research, you'll gain a clearer understanding of what's most interesting to your audience and what your content can best serve.

EXPLORING THE DOMAIN

Remember when you started at a new job? The exhilarating terror of parachuting into unfamiliar territory? Especially if you've worked in a digital agency or as a consultant (we've done both). Suddenly you're charged with delivering an app for car finance, health insurance, or bonsai care—or something else you know nothing about.

Scrabbling around, you turn to Google and start down a rabbit hole. Wikipedia articles. Blog posts. YouTube explainer videos. Piece by piece, you start to figure out just how this subject works. Don't look now, but you just did some domain research.

Research should be at the heart of any design project. Before you race headlong into making a solution, take the time to understand the problem. As Abraham Lincoln probably never said:

> Give me six hours to cut down a tree, and I'll spend the first four sharpening the axe.

Sharpening your subject knowledge empowers you to design better content and build finer products. You'll base your content inventory and navigation on the things people care about. You'll connect ideas in a way that helps people learn and understand. You'll give concepts the right names. You'll generally look like you know what you're talking about.

There's an old saying that still bounces around LinkedIn: "If you think hiring a professional was expensive, you should try hiring an amateur!" If you think doing up-front research costs time and money, try changing the course of a project once it hits engineering.

The start of any project is full of possibility. It could go in almost any direction. But back to Abe Lincoln and his axe-sharpening—do all the prep you can to set off on the right foot.

Early in the project you'll make a lot of mistakes. You'll have assumptions that aren't valid. Left unchecked, wrong thinking ends up codified in software. Once that happens, change management is expensive and time consuming, so much so that it often just doesn't happen. At that point, you can end up with a well-built product that fails to meet the needs of its audience—what research guru Tomer Sharon describes as "perfectly executing the wrong plan."

The start of the project is when it's cheapest to change your mind. During those early days, you'll change your mind a lot. Teams move faster when they're confident they're working on the right stuff. The domain research you'll carry out will set them up for success.

> **NOTE** Seriously, who takes six hours? And wasn't it Washington who cut down the tree? We're not sure he did that either. Still, Honest Abe was right on the money there. He could not tell a lie.

… there are known knowns; there are things we know we know. We also know there are known unknowns. That is to say, we know there are some things we do not know. But there are also unknown unknowns—the ones we don't know we don't know.

—Donald Rumsfeld

GETTING STARTED

Desk research is a great way to start. That's research from your desk, not researching desks. Unless of course your domain is furniture.

We bet you're already pretty good at Googling for stuff. It's a great way to soak yourself in the world of your subject. Vehicle maintenance, single-malt scotch whisky, pension planning—whatever your subject domain, there's a ton of material online. Start with Wikipedia articles, and for bonus points try the Talk tab on any Wikipedia page to see experts debate the finer points of a topic. For more specialist information, see if your domain has a professional membership association, such as the Institute of Electrical and Electronics Engineers or the Chartered Institute for Archaeologists. Those bodies make it their business to put out well-researched, authoritative information.

For an alternative to well-researched and authoritative information, visit discussion forums. That's unfair—some of them are pretty good. It's a chance to engage with experts and enthusiasts in their natural habitat. Forums and Facebook groups are where communities gather to discuss anything from skydiving to Beanie Babies. Read their conversations and see what conceptual objects emerge. Do they talk about equipment or techniques? Bible passages? Comic-book artists? Particular variants of the Android operating system? When people discuss a subject, they usually spend most of their time speaking about specific things or objects. Make a list of those things. Learn the shape of their world.

Becoming familiar with a topic helps you chart your territory. It gets you from not knowing what you don't know to knowing what you don't know. That's a good place to be. It means you have questions about how the subject works. What connects to what? How is one thing different from another? Now is the time to reach out to the people who really do know what they're talking about.

ASK THE EXPERTS

Subject-matter experts (SMEs) are everywhere. Remember that scene in *Raiders of the Lost Ark* where the G-men visit Dr. Indiana Jones to get the lowdown on the Ark of the Covenant? Indy is an SME. Now that's not to say all experts wear tweed jackets or lab coats. Many of them are much closer to home. They could even be your stakeholder or client.

What defines SMEs is their expertise in the subject domain. They might not know anything about app design, database tables, or content management systems, but by golly they've forgotten more about tropical fish keeping than you'll ever know. You need to get that knowledge out of their head and down on paper. It's the stuff designs are made of.

You're going to interview some domain experts. They'll tell you how the domain works. The most important concepts. The significant relationships. Any weird complexity that defies explanation. As the content specialist, you'll later help demystify and prioritize these concepts for your audience. But to do that, you first need to understand them. Ready to get started?

PREPARING FOR THE INTERVIEW

First you'll need to find appropriate interview subjects. Remember, you're look-ing for people who know the ins and outs of the subject domain. They could be your client, though people with some objectivity may work better. We've found that the person signing the checks sometimes has a specific agenda that can lead to a warped picture.

Interviewees could be:

- **Researchers.** These people have experience in gathering market intelli-gence. They'll have a good overview of the landscape.

- **Individual contributors.** If you want to get the bottom line on financial trading systems, ask financial traders. If you want to soak in the world of wine, talk to a sommelier. The folks on the front line have a more up-to-date understanding than anyone.

- **Founders.** Company founders know an awful lot. They've done a lot of background research to set up the company in the first place. They've studied the problem space—or in our case, the subject domain.

- **External experts.** Depending on the topic, some of the best authorities may lie outside your organization altogether. Who knows, maybe you do need a field trip to a dusty university to meet with a professor of archeology.

You'll need to interview many kinds of experts to build a complete picture of the subject domain. Get permission to talk to everyone, especially if they're not connected to your project. Ask your main client or stakeholder for a list of the best people to talk with. Make sure that approaching them isn't going to cause political friction.

When putting the ask out, explain what you're interested in learning from them. Explain that it's to help with your digital content project, not to gather feature requests. When you start talking to people in any organization, pretty soon you'll find folks with an axe to grind. They have been waiting for years for someone to ask about the website. And they have a mental list of all 97 things wrong with it. Politely explain that you'll be happy to make a note of all 97. But this round of research is for learning about the subject. They'll later get their chance to write a letter to Santa.

Prepare for each interview by doing desk research in advance. Get a sense of the subject so that you can drive the conversation. Gather questions about things you need them to explain. Decide how broad you'd like the conversation to go. Are you asking them to tell you all about astronomy as a whole, or are you focusing only on its observational branch?

You're going in to learn. Although a little foreknowledge is great for giving you context, this isn't the time to show off how much you know. Practice professional naiveté; pretend you don't know and let them tell you. "Oh, I didn't know that!" you'll lie. "So does that mean that cubism is an art *movement* rather than an art *style*?" (even though you totally looked it up on Wikipedia beforehand). Experts may even offer conflicting advice. The world is messy, and knowledge isn't clean. If what you hear contradicts what you understand, explore that further. You may find yourself uncovering diverse viewpoints that somehow need to be expressed in your product.

If you can, visit your SME where they're most comfortable talking about their expertise. Phone calls and Skype are convenient, but nothing beats what researchers call "contextual inquiry." Interview subjects tend to open up more if they're on their own turf. They have all their contextual cues around them. They're relying less on memory alone.

CONDUCTING THE INTERVIEW

Take along a few things to help you out:

■ A reliable audio recording device

■ Notepad, pencil, eraser, and sticky notes

■ Printouts of anything that you want to ask more about

TIP If you're using a recording app on your phone, make sure calls, messages, or push alerts don't interfere with the recording.

Schedule the interview for no more than one hour. Anything longer can be off-putting to the interviewee. You're going to be pretty focused, and maintaining concentration beyond an hour is difficult. Budget your time carefully:

- **Introduction (5 minutes).** During the introduction, you explain who you are and why you're there. Make sure they know that you've come to learn from their expertise.

- **Set context (5 minutes).** Here you'll explain that you're trying to understand the domain, which is why you're asking super-specific questions. Ask also if they have any questions for you before you get started.

- **Main interview (30 minutes).** During this time, you get down to what you came for. Ask broad questions to get the interviewee's overview of a topic; then dive into the details. It's not every day someone gets asked for a complete braindump. Use your first few questions to get them into the flow. If your interviewee is struggling, lean on your preparatory research to ask some clarifying questions. For example, "I was doing some reading and got confused about the difference between a hurricane and a cyclone. Could you help me understand?" If they're finding it hard to verbalize their answers, suggest that they try to draw it in whatever way makes sense to them.

  Listen for the concepts—the nouns—they reference. Make sure to capture these in your notes, and probe further about anything that's unclear. To make the most of the interview, you want to come away with a list of the subject's principal concepts and an understanding of how they connect.

- **Clarify (13 minutes).** Start your wrap-up by summarizing your conversation. Repeat back your understanding and correct any errors. If you've sketched out any visual representation of the domain, review it together.

- **Thanks (2 minutes).** Thank them for their time. Explain that their expertise helps make a better product. If they have a lot more to say, ask if you can schedule another session. Ask if they can recommend other experts to speak with and whether they'd make an introduction. If they turn out to be an awesome expert, ask if they'd be willing to take part in a workshop session later in the project (more about that in Chapter 5).

- **The Columbo moment (5 minutes).** Try to "end" the interview at least five minutes early. This gives time for something that will be familiar to fans of TV detective Columbo. The crumpled police lieutenant would interview a suspect. He'd then make as if to leave, before turning back with an innocent-but-crucial "oh, just one more thing…." With your interview subject, it'll be the other way around. As you pack up and head for the door, your interviewee will get a flash of inspiration. They'll explain some crucial detail that would otherwise get missed. This doesn't always happen, but expect the unexpected.

This should go without saying, but be on time and be courteous. These folks aren't part of your project team. They don't have to help you out, so be nice. Tell them you heard that they're the expert in this subject (it always pays to butter them up). Tell them that you need their help in explaining things step by step:

```
FADE IN:

INT: Event planning office. Day.

Coffee-ringed papers litter every desk. A busy whiteboard
looms large, plastered with sticky notes and graffitied with
gridlines. Poster mock-ups peel from the walls. Phones ring in
the background, the soundtrack to perpetual urgency.

                          YOU
          Thanks so much for your time! My name is Carrie,
          and I'm working on content for the new IA Summit
          website. You're chairing the event. I heard you
          know everything there is to know, so I was hoping
          to spend the next hour picking your brain. This
          isn't the conversation where we talk about what
          should go on the website. This is just to help me
          understand how this event works so that I can plan
          the content. If it's okay, I'd like to record the
          conversation so I don't have to take quite so many
          notes.

          So please, tell me about the IA Summit.

                        EXPERT
          Sure. Gosh. Where to begin. Well, we're currently
          planning next year's event, which will be at the
          Hilton in Chicago. Right now, I've just signed one
          of our keynote speakers, which I'm pumped about.
```

They've never spoken at the event before. Over
there you'll see Dalia, my co-chair. She's chasing
up some of our volunteers to help with promotion.
It's a busy time for us, as our call for papers
has closed now. We need our reviewers to help
select which talks and workshops and stuff go into
each program track.

*Whoa, let's back up a second. Your expert has just thrown a bunch of useful
information at you. But understandably, it's weighted toward the things they're
thinking about right now, so it comes out a little jumbled. Still, it's more than
enough to start asking questions:*

>   YOU
> You said next year's event is in Chicago. Is there
> an IA Summit every year? Is it always in Chicago?

>   EXPERT
> Yes, there's an event once every year. It's always
> in a different city somewhere in North America.
> Last year we were at the Hyatt in Vancouver.

>   YOU
> So it's always in a hotel? Does that make it
> easier to keep everyone together?

>   EXPERT
> Most always in a hotel, yes. It means they have
> conference facilities already set up. And rooms,
> of course. Wherever we hold the event, we always
> manage to get a discounted rate at a downtown
> hotel.

>   YOU
> I didn't realize there was more than one co-chair!
> Are you all volunteers?

>   EXPERT
> Oh, no one gets paid—I wish we did! So we need
> a bunch of people helping out. There are three
> co-chairs—we are replaced every year. There're
> also people like the curation manager and the
> experience director. And the people who review
> submissions. Last year I managed the review
> process, so I know how tricky that is.

> YOU
>
> Okay, so there are some different roles filled each year. And sometimes the same person might have one role one year and a different role the following year?

> EXPERT
>
> Yeah, they might even wear a few different hats for the same event—just depends on how many volunteers we get. Some previous attendees or speakers are now getting more involved in organizing.

Interesting. So now you know it's an annual event, with a different location each year—usually in a hotel, because they need conference facilities and attendee accommodation. There are several roles associated with each event, and the same person might have one or more roles for a given event. Let's keep going:

> YOU
>
> You mentioned the reviewers were planning the program tracks. How does that work?

> EXPERT
>
> Every conference has some sessions—talks, shorter talks, and hands-on stuff. Reviewers decide which session submissions make the cut. They plan out the main three days. Each day starts with a keynote, then splits into three tracks. Attendees choose whether they want to see more academic or practical talks. We all come together again at the end of the day for our happy hour. On Saturday night, we'll have karaoke too, assuming we can get a sponsor. Oh, I forgot! Before the main conference, we have a couple of days of pre-conference workshops.

> YOU
>
> Tell me more about the tracks. Can any kind of session go in any of the tracks? What about the keynote and the social events?

> EXPERT
>
> Yes. We try to mix up different session formats in each track. The 5-minute lightning talks were popular last year, so we're doing those again.

```
For the keynotes and socials, everyone's invited.
It's not just keynotes either. We've started doing
things like morning yoga. But doing that extra
stuff depends on sponsorship.

                    YOU
Can a sponsor only sponsor a social session?

                  EXPERT
We'll gladly take their money for any kind of
session! Often they sponsor specific social
sessions, like the happy hour. But sometimes they
just give money to the event generally...
```

As you chat, tease out information to give structure to your understanding of the domain. By asking clarifying questions, you expose the inherent logic and business rules. You'll later express these through content and interface design. Keep digging into areas of complexity:

- Are speaker and keynote speaker two different roles?

- Can organizers also be speakers at the same event?

- If each conference is an "event," what do you call the IA Summit as a whole?

- How are pre-conference workshops different from main conference sessions?

Your goal is to come out of the interview with a list of terms. You should understand what each of those terms means (TABLE 4.1) and how they fit together.

TABLE 4.1 **TERMS AND DEFINITIONS**

TERM	DEFINITION
Brand	The overall IA Summit brand, distinct from specific conference events.
Event	The 2016 IA Summit is an event.
Location	Place the event is held. Different city each year.
Venue	Within the location, a specific venue (usually a hotel) houses the event.
Hotel	The "official" hotel for attendee accommodation. Usually this is the same as the event venue, though not necessarily.
Person	An individual associated with one or more events.

(continues)

TABLE 4.1 **TERMS AND DEFINITIONS** *(continued)*

TERM	DEFINITION
Role	The specific role (such as speaker, co-chair, or volunteer) a person has within an event. A person may hold one or more roles for the same event.
Topic	May refer to the subject theme of a specific session or of an overall event.
Session	A specific occurrence within an event, such as a workshop or social.
Session format	The type of session, such as 45-minute talk, social, or workshop.
Track	A thematic grouping of sessions.
Sponsor	Company that sponsors (contributes financially to) an event or session.

Soon you'll use these concepts to construct an abstract model of the subject domain. We've found, though, that it's often difficult to get people to think at this level. If interviewing alone isn't getting you the answers you need, try using an exercise.

CONDUCTING A CASUAL CARD SORT

A card sort is a popular exercise for helping people categorize information. Take a set of index cards with you to the interview. On each, write down one concept from the subject domain (you may have gleaned these from previous interviews). Ask your interviewee to arrange the cards in a way that makes sense to them. This may be in piles of related things or by just placing related things close to each other. If they want to, let them create new cards, remove cards, or rename existing ones. As they go along, ask them to "think aloud" and explain their decision process. In truth, the cards themselves aren't important. They're just physical stimuli to help your participant think and talk aloud about the subject's structure.

SKETCHING A MENTAL MODEL

Some people express themselves better visually rather than verbally. Take a drawing pad and some sticky notes to the interview. As you chat, start to jot down the concepts you hear, drawing lines to connect related concepts. You're making a "mind map." Show your interviewee what you're doing. Have them help you sketch (**FIGURE 4.2**). Work together to draw a visual representation of the domain. In Chapter 5, we'll develop this idea as you build a detailed domain model.

FIGURE 4.2
Collaborative sketching of a mental model.

TALKING TO THE USERS

Those domain experts know their stuff, don't they? It's so useful to draw on their experience and soak up their knowledge. But it's not the whole story. Unless you're making a product for those experts, you have a whole other group to consider: your audience.

Who are the target users of your product? Who's the audience for your content? These are the folks your work serves. Not the client. Not the boardroom. Content is for use. Anyone engaging with your product does so because they have underlying needs and questions. Maybe they need to understand mortgages. Perhaps they're looking to restore a vintage sports car. Could be they're just dying to know what cool and funny baby-panda-on-a-slide videos are out there.

Go talk with them. Your experts have armed you with enough context to understand the subject. When you listen to users enthuse, you'll have at least some idea of what they're talking about. You'll find their take on the subject a little different from the SMEs'.

DIFFERENT TERMS

Depending on the subject, a correct "expert" term may differ from common usage. What we might call a "magic trick" is something a professional magician would term an "illusion" or "effect." The wonderful-sounding "grawlix" helps comic-book artists cover up their @#$%&!-ing foul language. Building a medical symptom checker? Maybe don't file content under "xerostomiath" if your general reader wants help with plain ol' "cotton-mouth."

Differences matter. They tell us where the worldview of the expert diverges from the view of the audience. It's not always as simple as a one-for-one substitution of terms. Sometimes what looks like one concept unpacks into several under expert scrutiny. We assumed a conference had a bunch of associated speakers. Then we learned about speakers, keynotes, hosts, and a bunch of other volunteer roles.

DIFFERENT LEVELS OF DETAIL

Once, we were developing an app for a video game store. We wanted to learn about game consoles, so we engaged with a community of collectors. These guys knew everything, from the age of Atari to the present day. We knew there were different consoles released by manufacturers (we know our Super NES from our Wii), but we learned that almost every console had many model variants during its lifetime. And that some of those variants were available in different limited editions. Yet when we spoke to casual video game enthusiasts, none of those details came up. Oh sure, they'd argue the relative merits of PlayStation versus Xbox. But to them, these were just competing formats in the same way people once compared VHS and Betamax. Ask your parents.

Experts help us go deep on the fascinating nuances of a subject, but users remind us what's important. Remember that your product exists to respect and reflect the interests of your audience. Cross-reference information from both parties. Aim for a product that balances expert authority with audience-appropriateness. Experts map the world; users mark the points of interest.

EXISTING RESEARCH

Every organization has a ton of research material, even if they don't know it. Audience segmentation reports. Focus group studies. Even sales figures. There are all kinds of places to find out what's working for the business and what's not. Stuff to help you figure out who the customers are and what they need. And many organizations have whole departments dedicated to helping customers get what they need. They call them customer service teams. These folks aren't without their own bias (recent complaints from shouty or important customers have a habit of becoming high-priority feature requests), but still they're a valuable source of customer insight.

Website analytics can be a great way to learn your users' language. If people visited you by entering a search query on Google, which terms did they use? If your site has its own search, you can go further still. When people type into that search box, they're telling you the content they want and the terms they use to describe it. Look for the trends there and add them to the list of inputs that inform your terminology decisions.

OVERCOMING OBJECTIONS

The path to enlightenment never did run smooth. You'd think any organization would fall over themselves to do as much research as possible. Surely it's obvious that gathering intel helps prevent major disasters further down the line. "Measure twice, cut once" and all that.

No-brainer, right? You'd be surprised.

One of the most common hurdles to overcome in a digital project is convincing stakeholders to invest in up-front research.

Here's your handy guide to the more popular objections you may encounter:

We already know what our customers want.

Despite hiring you to deliver valuable content, stakeholders still insist they know best. Fine, start there. Get a list of requests and treat them as assumptions. Assumptions are there to be challenged or confirmed. Domain research confirms whether experts and users agree with your stakeholders about what's important.

Say, "All your suggestions are interesting. We don't have budget to do everything. Let me talk to the customers to make sure we're not spending money on the wrong stuff."

We don't want to bother anyone.

This happens a lot, especially if you're an agency engaging with a client company. The implicit translation is "we don't want *you* bothering anyone." It's as though the company is afraid of looking vulnerable in front of its own customers. Here are a couple of lines to try:

"This app we're making needs to pay for itself by reducing calls to the support center. Let's find out what kind of support customers need most. Then I can provide the right content to meet your goals."

"To make you a great website, I need to understand your business. We can decide on what that looks like later. For now, let's talk to some people from around the business to figure out how everything works."

It will take too long.

As opposed to what? Diving straight in without a clue? Maybe your stakeholder got burned by a six-month research project that led to nothing but a report. That report currently resides unread at the bottom of everyone's drawer. But you're asking for only a few weeks (maybe even a few days) to lay the groundwork for the whole project. Tell them this:

"It's great that you're eager to get started. I want to make sure we lay the right foundations before we start building. Let me put time in your diary for us to chat. In the meantime, I'll reach out to other folks around the business. I want to get a real understanding of what happens here."

It will hold up engineering.

We truly, madly, deeply love engineers. They're the people who make the rubber meet the road. But sometimes they're treated like a marching army who must never stop for anything or anyone. (If only the rest of us commanded that much respect.) If you're treating your most expensive people with such care, you should want to point them at the right problem. Give this line a whirl:

"I want to get engineering involved! This kind of planning could use their expertise in how to structure information. What I'm calling 'research' is really how we get them what they need to build the data model."

By the way, that's completely true. Figuring out the subject domain informs the model you'll design to support content in your database or CMS. In fact, engineers have been some of our most supportive allies in this process. More on that in Chapter 5.

We're doing Agile development.

The Agile manifesto for software development favors "responding to change over following a plan." For some teams, that can mean that anything that smells like planning gets dismissed out of hand. But even the smartest Agile teams don't dive into development without a clue about what they're trying to achieve. Instead, they develop a working hypothesis. You're proposing just enough research to get them started.

"I believe that using structured content will make the product more useful and usable. If we build for the right mental model, we're investing effort in a scalable content framework. That's much more efficient than making one-off, throwaway microsites."

Agile teams may start by building something smaller, sooner. Starting with a small, structured content prototype, they'll follow the same process of research and discovery and funnel everything they learn into a new and improved prototype.

It will be too expensive.

Not nearly as expensive as leaping into interface design and engineering without a plan. Since good preparation is the basis of any project, we're not sure that even the stakeholders who make this argument believe it. Still, prepare to defend your ground:

"As you know, cost and complexity increase the further you get into a project. I'm trying to contain costs by preventing any rework due to assumptions that turn out to be incorrect. This is perhaps the cheapest way of preventing expense later."

Don't judge your stakeholders too harshly for questioning the need for research. They're paying for the creation of a digital product. Their mental picture of that creation may be more around pixels and code than Dictaphones and transcripts. Don't be tempted to cast them in the role of antagonist. Mostly, they're not the archetypal "client from hell" who's there to reduce you to a human mouse pointer and execute their "make the logo bigger" ideas. They're just people. Like you, they have a job to do, and they're held to account for success. Maybe they have good reason to contain costs. Certainly, they're apt to ask questions about the process. You're there to help them understand.

The best way to frame this research is not as a preliminary warm-up to the main event. Pitch it as the start of the design process itself, which it is. By this point, you've convinced your stakeholders of a structured content-first approach. They understand that when you say "design," you're not just talking about user interfaces. Designing structure begins with figuring out the things to be structured and the ways that they connect.

DEFINING PROBLEMS BEFORE SOLUTIONS

Domain research has a different focus than the UX research you may have encountered before. A good UX researcher attempts to understand user needs and clarify business requirements. Their goal is to understand the problem before the team sets about designing a solution. UX research reveals a product's most-used features and pain points. It shows the broader context that leads people to engage with your product in the first place.

We could have written a whole book on research alone. But it would have been nowhere near as good as Steve Portigal's *Interviewing Users* (Rosenfeld Media) or Erika Hall's *Just Enough Research* (A Book Apart). Instead, we've focused on the exercise of gathering information about your subject domain.

Domain research lays the groundwork for content structure. Your content implicitly or explicitly supports the concepts and relationships inherent in a topic. These are the foundations that drive your structural design.

Most of the time, you're not designing for yourself. Your expertise is in making useful, usable digital products—and knowing who to lean on for insight. Domain experts help you understand the rules, exceptions, and tricky parts of your subject. Users tell you what's most important to cover. As we'll go on to explore, this research funnels into the construction of a domain model. In turn, this model guides how you'll segment and structure content. Up-front research may seem time-consuming, but you need it to make sure your product serves the real-world domain. Addressing misunderstandings during research is much, much cheaper than waiting until later.

Domain research exposes the territory you intend to map. Sharing this research with stakeholders shows them where you're headed. This may lead to discussion, negotiation, or even heated debate over the boundaries of the subject area. Better that this happens now rather than later. As you align on the subject domain, you fix on a crucial point of agreement. Even if you decide not to follow a structured content approach, do yourself a favor and get everyone on your team to agree on the shape of the domain. It's like a save point in a videogame. No matter how much you argue later about the specifics of content or interface design, there's always a safe place to get back to. But more on that teamwork in Chapter 5.

Overcoming your own bias, or that of your stakeholders, is always challenging. You'll likely come to the project with an idea of how it should turn out. That's no bad thing, but see it for what it is—an assumption about what success looks like. Research helps you challenge your assumptions and make adjustments. Research gets you answers. But it also uncovers new questions. You're asking your experts and users to tell you how their world works. Their answers can be unexpected, and that gives more and more insight into the problem space.

In practice, your research interviews will be a little messy. Often, your experts are also stakeholders. Your users may be keener to talk feature requests than to analyze the components of a subject. Conversations will mix domain research with a broader exploration of needs and opportunities. Keeping people on-topic is difficult. Recognize that every critique or request is a way of people expressing what's important to them. Probe deeper and find the desire hiding behind the feature suggestion.

Through domain research, you'll listen and observe. You'll build understanding. You'll build relationships with people you can call on again throughout the project. You'll gain empathy for your users, your experts, and, above all, the subject itself.

Uncovering Domain Complexity

AN INTERVIEW WITH ELLEN DE VRIES

Ellen De Vries is a content strategist at the design agency Clearleft. She is fascinated by the language people use to collaborate and the taxonomies and techniques needed to wrestle the constraints of resources, time, physics, and CMS fields.

Ellen, can you tell us about the vocabulary dump technique you have used to uncover domain complexity?

When the domain is unwieldy and complex, when stakeholders are so diverse they don't understand one another's vocabularies, and when your subject matter experts are dropping acronyms into the conversations like confetti, it might be time to create an energized vocabulary dump.

One of Clearleft's founders, Andy Budd, invited a diverse group of artificial intelligence experts—from radio presenters to sci-fi authors to robot researchers—to a retreat where the movie *Ex Machina* was filmed, in remotest Norway. It became apparent to me (as a facilitator and non-expert) that the AI (artificial intelligence) subject domain is vast. The vocabularies are complex, and the conversations have interesting themes: from dystopian futures to human versus non-humanoid robot design.

To create divergence in the conversation and reflect diversity in the group, our team made a vocabulary dump. It's a simple tool for facilitating conversations with subject matter experts or between people who need to understand one another's perspectives. Sticky notes helped us offload all the associative words related to AI. First stuck randomly on the cabin wall, the notes were soon clustered into nouns, verbs, and adjectives (with an additional category for "retro-nouns," which need qualification, like digital pencil or self-driving car). With the vocabulary captured, some of the team reorganized the notes to uncover emergent themes.

The exercise made clear to everyone the vast scale of the domain and where there was convergence in expertise. It highlighted the need to define complex, vague, or obfuscatory terms and acronyms. But it opened up discussion about meaning and possibility and encouraged us to investigate the breadth of the domain.

Developing a shared vocabulary sparks deeper conversations. It helps people question assumptions, articulate meaning, and align understanding. Seeking clear definitions is a fruitful way for the facilitator and participants to get closer to the subject matter.

CHAPTER 5

CREATING A DOMAIN MODEL

So you had some great introductory conversations with your subject-matter experts and target audiences. You listened. You asked probing questions. You've taken your first step into the larger world of your subject domain. Fascinating, isn't it? Taking apart a topic and seeing how it all works is one of the most exciting parts of the design process. Defining a list of terms is the first step to gaining understanding. The next step is figuring out how those terms relate. We need a way to explore and communicate how the whole subject hangs together.

HOW DO WE MAKE THE CONNECTIONS?

Enter the *domain model*—a conceptual model of the subject domain. It shows the concepts found in that domain and the specific relationships between them. Hang out with software engineers and you might see them use entity-relationship diagrams (ERDs) to design complex systems such as database architectures. The diagram names each part of the system, defines the properties that make up each part, and shows the connections between all the parts.

In his book *Domain-Driven Design: Tackling Complexity at the Heart of Software*, Eric Evans co-opts the ERD to model a subject. He uses the example of air-traffic control systems, mapping out the complexities of flights, routes, and flight plans. In Eric's book, domain modeling supports a software development process. Teams split the software project into parts, conforming to subsections of the domain.

If you're not a software engineer, you may have tuned out already. But it's okay—the domain model itself isn't technical or scary at all. It's just a way of drawing on paper the things you already know. We've used domain modeling to help us make sure our content addresses user needs. It helps us chop up that content into the most useful and interesting parts. And it helps us structure and present content to different audiences on different devices.

Done right, the domain model is one of the most pivotal artifacts of any content project, informing everyone's work. Every design, every piece of content, and all code can be traced back to the model. Getting alignment on the model helps your team get passionate about the subject. Support that subject with content and software, and you help your audience understand and explore what they care about.

As you'll see, the model is structural, so it's easy to mistake it for a fancy version of a site map. But this isn't in itself a blueprint for how the parts of your digital product are arranged. In fact, free your mind from thoughts of digital products altogether. The domain model maps your subject, not your website.

CONNECTING CONCEPTS

Modeling starts by connecting two or more concepts. Within a domain model, each concept is called a *domain object*. From your research, you'll already have a good idea of what the major domain objects will be.

In Chapter 4, we explored the subject domain of the IA Summit conference. (Don't worry if conferences aren't your bag; there are more examples coming up.) One of the main objects was `Person` (**FIGURE 5.1**). A person is an honest-to-goodness rational human being. (Well, sometimes conference planning makes irrational beings of all of us, but that's another story.) The domain objects build a picture of the subject. So each object represents a real-world concept.

FIGURE 5.1
A domain object.

Why `Person` and not something like `Speaker`? Many people involved in the conference aren't speakers. They might be the conference co-chair or the host of a social event. Even the folks who run hands-on workshops aren't strictly "speakers." For now, `Person` it is. Object names are singular (so `Person`, not `People`) because the model shows how one example of each object relates to one example of another object.

Another object is `Session`, which covers things like 45-minute lectures, workshops, 5-minute lightning talks, and even social sessions, such as the karaoke night. Each session is associated with at least one person (**FIGURE 5.2**), who is usually the speaker or host of that session.

FIGURE 5.2
Adding another object.

Why go with `Session` for everything rather than using a bunch of different objects, like `Social`, `Lecture`, and `Workshop`? We want the model to be reusable and flexible and document only the things that remain true over time. The IA Summit experiments with different types of sessions each year. Who knew a 6 a.m. fun run would catch on?

Regardless of the type of session, the relationship to `Person` remains the same. `Session` is flexible enough to work for any type of session we plan. So let's add another object to express that each session has a type: `Session Format` (**FIGURE 5.3**).

FIGURE 5.3
Another object.

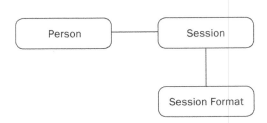

Again, we're being flexible. `Session Format` is broad enough to cover everything from the academic round table to the social board-game evening. And on and on we go, adding more related objects until a comprehensive model emerges.

Objects vs. Instances

Remember, you want this model to be reusable, so be careful to distinguish between domain objects and *instances* of those objects. An instance is a specific example of the concept represented by the domain object. Let's say you are doing something about movies and have a domain object of `Character`. Forrest Gump would be an example—or *instance*—of that object. You can't put Forrest directly into the model as an object, because he's not reusable. If you later want to add Lieutenant Dan, you'd need a whole other object. So domain objects are general forms designed to cope with many instance examples, many of which aren't known in advance. You might say they're like a box of chocolates.

Sometimes it's easy to mistake an instance for an object. In one of the first drafts of the IA Summit conference model, we used the object `Hotel`. This represented the place where the conference was held, usually one of the more soul-sucking U.S. chain hotels. Oh, except that one time when it was in a convention center. Or that time they had to split up sessions at different lecture theaters all over town. Damn—`Hotel` doesn't cut it as a domain object after all. What you want is `Venue`. Far more flexible. You can even reuse that same object to describe the individual rooms for each session.

Note that the model *does* include a `Hotel` object, but that refers to the official accommodation for attendees. We think that will always be a hotel, but who knows? Maybe that hipster cabin-in-the-woods maker-hacker/bike-repair event could fly.

It takes a little forward thinking to figure out what's likely to change over time. But by designing for change up front, you'll make a more scalable product.

FORMING MEANINGFUL RELATIONSHIPS

Domain models use the relationships between concepts to build understanding. Those boxes in the diagrams are super important. More important still are the lines that connect them. When you connected that `Person` object to the `Session` object, you understood why you did it. But to anyone else reading the model, it's just a line. Maybe you should give it a name.

Relationships have values. A moon – orbits – a planet. The author – wrote – the novel. The cat – sits on – the mat. These describe the nature of the relationship. If domain objects are nouns, then relationship values are the verbs that connect them. Or to return to vague memories of English class:

Subject – Predicate – Object

For the `Person-Session` relationship, you need to define what a `Person` does to a `Session` (or, if you prefer, what a `Session` has in store for a `Person`). For now, let's keep it simple and assume you're dealing only with the session host. `Host` seems like a good term that works for the person who runs lectures, workshops, or social sessions (**FIGURE 5.4**). So let's say:

FIGURE 5.4 Building a relationship between objects.

Just like that, the relationship has a value. It tells everyone exactly why that poor `Person` is forever shackled to the `Session`. Oh, and that weird style for `hostedBy` is deliberate. It's called camel case, and it's a common convention to maintain a one-word name. That helps the terms you define be carried through to database design.

Which way around should you make your relationship? Should you assert that a hotel has a restaurant? Or is it better to say that the restaurant is located in the hotel? Actually, it doesn't matter too much in the model, but try to be consistent. We prefer to standardize on the idea that a larger concept contains a smaller one. The hotel has a restaurant, but the restaurant doesn't have a hotel.

When you publish your content, you can use relationship values to link resources together. Remember the bad old days of web design? Those right-hand columns filled with "related links"? Related how, exactly? The links never told us. But by explicitly defining the relationship in the model, your links can convey more meaning. A page about a hotel can show its restaurants.

A page about a particular restaurant can show which hotel it's located in. A page profiling a person could connect automatically to every session the person has ever hosted. Should any person later change their name, or a session switch to a different host, then that information would be updated everywhere.

Expressing relationships in the domain model completes the picture of how one concept connects to another. Soon these relationships will inform the design of your content management system (CMS). Eventually they will guide your interface navigation. Most importantly, they show the team, and the audience, how your world joins up.

BREAKING DOWN A MODEL

FIGURE 5.5 is the complete domain model we created for the IA Summit conference. It's made up of domain objects and relationship values. Let's go through it piece by piece.

FIGURE 5.5 IA Summit conference domain model.

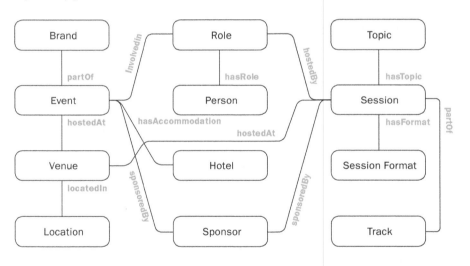

The Event refers to the specific conference event. We first worked on the 2015 IA Summit, in Minneapolis, but we could reuse this model for every future summit (or every previous event, dating back to 2000).

Each event belongs to the master conference Brand—in our case, the IA Summit. There are a few concepts associated with the brand as a whole (such as its mission, vision, and values). It's useful to distinguish the brand from individual events.

We hold the event in a specific Venue. That venue has a real-world Location, which is useful to include to give people a sense of physical spaces relative to each other.

A Person is associated with an event. But not all associations are the same. There are session hosts, keynote speakers, volunteers, chairpeople, committee members, and more. We called each of these a Role. To capture this in the model, we decided that a Role is associated with an Event and that each Role is filled by a Person.

Over time, the same person may be associated with many events and roles. Maybe this year they're a volunteer. Next year they could host a session. Perhaps one day, they are a keynote speaker. Their role relative to each event would change, but they're still the same person. Even within a single event, they may wear many hats. Identifying them as the same person means we can get the content management system to connect related sessions and roles. And now we have a useful way to showcase each person's illustrious speaking career.

Each Session is associated with an Event. A Session has a Session Format (for example, lecture, workshop, and social) and an associated Venue (such as a ballroom, lecture theater, or yurt). Note that here we're reusing the Venue domain object that we associated with the event itself. Does this mean they have to hold the same value? Nope! The fact that a Venue object is associated with both the Session object and the Event object takes care of both use cases. Whether it houses a single talk or an entire conference, the Venue object is defined in the same way.

A Session may cover a specific Topic, which we'll use to help curate the speaking program. Our event is multi-track, meaning that several sessions run concurrently and attendees choose their poison. Each session belongs to exactly one Track.

The event can have a Sponsor. More than one, we hope. Someone's got to pay for those happy hours. An individual session may also be sponsored, especially that happy hour, brought to you through the kind generosity of Pearson Education. (See how good that sounds? Can we have our money now?)

And that's it! Although simple, it's powerful enough to guide the planning and structure of content across an entire series of conference events. It captures connections between people and ideas, within an event and across the years.

NOTE So it turns out we were wrong before to associate Person directly with Session! It's more correct to assert that a Person holds the Role of Host and that it's actually the Role that is associated with the Session. But that's okay—revisions like this happen all the time in modeling, as you think about specific use cases and adapt your model accordingly.

Maybe your model for this domain would look different, and that's fine. We had some great debates over ours. Should a `Session` and an `Event` be different things? Maybe we could have reused the `Event` object to have events *within* events. Were `Session Format` and `Topic` useful enough to define as fully fledged domain objects? Each successive pass over the model brings opportunities to refine and simplify.

There's no right answer. Your model is your best take on capturing the subject domain. Like any model, it's an abstraction from the specifics of reality. Those specifics can be expressed in more than one way. As the grunt said of Camelot in *Monty Python and the Holy Grail*, it's only a model.

MODELING IS TEAMWORK

Everyone on your team should develop the model together. Designer, engineer, content strategist, researcher, product manager—everyone. You're building a common vision of your subject domain. To set up your project for success, you must, must, *must* align on that vision. If the team can agree on nothing else later on, at least agree on this.

Getting buy-in from a team requires their participation. When a teammate has to later interpret what's documented, they can go off script, especially in areas where they don't agree. A lack of alignment starts tremors that reverberate throughout the product design. Conceptual issues magnify when codified into database tables, content strategies, and information architecture. It's better to get it right now, while it's still just boxes and arrows on paper.

Discuss your research. Develop a model that best serves the subject, the audiences, the stakeholders, and you as a team. Conversations uncover complexity. Solutions are better when you question assumptions and fold new perspectives into the mix.

USING THE STICKY NOTE METHOD

Get a room. A big room, with a large table. Enough to take a team of four to six people. Enough to spread out and make a mess. Grab your designers, engineers, writers, stakeholders, experts, users. Take cupcakes and Haribo. You're going to need some teamwork.

You will need

- A few large sheets of paper (flip chart paper is great)

- A stack of sticky notes

- Sharpies or other pens

- The domain knowledge gleaned from your research

- A willingness to discuss and debate the domain

On each sticky note write the name of a domain object. That in itself should get the conversation started. Once you agree on a valid object and align on a name, stick it on the big sheet of paper. Don't worry—this decision isn't final. You're going to move a lot of things around before you're finished.

Repeat for every domain object. Don't worry where you stick them on the paper right now. You'll be doing a lot of repositioning as you figure out how things fit together.

As you place each object, discuss what it is and how it relates to other objects. Do you have the right object name? If not, toss the note and write a new one. Sticky notes are cheap.

Once you have your objects down, move them around to place related objects together. It doesn't have to be perfect. Most first-draft domain models are messy. Move things around and talk about them. You might find you need an extra object or realize an existing object is unnecessary. The sticky notes and wastepaper basket are your friends.

Got a bunch of objects down on paper? Great! Now for the part that seems to scare people. Honestly, we've done this exercise in workshops and seen folks put off this step for as long as they can. Take a pen, and draw a line on the paper to connect two of the domain objects. Then write on the line a label to describe the relationship. Remember that sometimes those relationships aren't thrilling (`Recipe – hasIngredient – Ingredient`), but label them anyway.

Keep going, connecting all your domain objects. After the commitment-free ease of sticky notes, drawing black lines with a Sharpie feels horribly permanent. It's okay—this is still your rough, throwaway draft. It's meant to be messy. Mistakes can even be helpful, signaling some bit of domain complexity to tease out.

Once you're done, test-drive the model with different instance examples. Make sure everything holds up. Where you need a little tuning, make some quick fixes with the sticky notes.

Keeping everything on paper helps the exercise feel interactive. Sometimes we just think better about this stuff when we're using our hands and moving around. Keeping it rough stops things from feeling too technical or intimidating (FIGURE 5.6). It gives everyone permission to make mistakes. Above all, this process is a way of helping the team come together and explore the domain. The conversations that come from modeling are as least as important as the model itself. It's the activity, not the artifact, that matters most.

FIGURE 5.6 Keeping modeling messy with sticky notes and Sharpies.

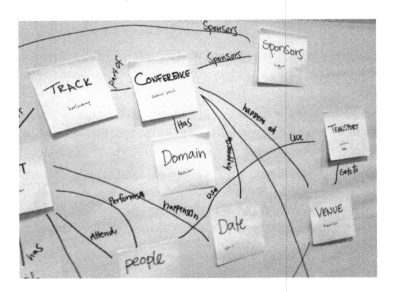

AGREEING ON YOUR DOMAIN

We often run workshops to help people get the hang of domain modeling. Usually we ask teams to pick their own subject. Once a team chose to model the TV show *Twin Peaks*. They started well, defining objects like Character and Episode. Then things started getting complicated. Should they model "inside" the universe (characters, interactions, motivations, places, and plot events) or "outside" the universe (episodes, broadcasts, movies, and DVD releases)? It quickly became as convoluted as the show itself.

Sometimes your team's mental models need alignment. Understand and agree about up front exactly what you're trying to capture. Modeling Health Care would take you in a different direction than modeling Medicine. Without team alignment on the domain, you'll find it hard to express the domain as a model. If you're having a lot of disagreements while modeling, wind things back. Make sure you all have the same domain in mind.

Discuss the subject domain your business operates in. If you sell concert tickets, serve your audience by modeling Live Music. If you work on a savings app, maybe it's Personal Finance. Set that expectation early on. There's a huge difference between modeling Live Music and attempting Music as a whole. Remember that your audience's interest doesn't begin and end with your business proposition. They're interacting with your business because of their interest in a broader topic. Just what is that topic? And how can you better serve them by supporting it?

Remember that your audience's interest doesn't begin and end with your business proposition. They're interacting with your business because of their interest in a broader topic.

Consider what's actually useful to your audience. If we modeled Road Tripping, we'd stick to `Routes`, `Cities`, `Vehicles`, and `Points of Interest`, and not so much the Interstate Highway Act, road composition, or gas consumption. But your mileage may vary.

Modeling resists constraint because all knowledge is fundamentally connected. In our Road Tripping example, it would be easy and reasonable to throw in the `Vehicle` object. That might have a `Vehicle Type`. Pretty soon you're down a rabbit hole, throwing in objects like `Manufacturer`, `Engine`, and `Model Variant`. This has drifted into the domain of `Automobiles` and lost sight of what's most compelling to the audience and business.

MAKING GOOD DOMAIN OBJECTS

Our chosen subject contains abstract concepts we captured as domain objects. But knowing what makes a good object can be tough. So here's a spoiler for the next chapter: Domain objects contain *attributes*. They are the atoms in the molecule, the protons in the atom, or something. (Don't ask us to model Chemistry.)

For example, `Person` is a great object for our IA Summit domain. But we want our person to have a name, a headshot photo, a biography, and maybe even a link to their blog. Are these things also domain objects? Not necessarily. Most likely they're just descriptive attributes of that domain object. These attributes don't have to appear in your domain model. You'll express them later in the detailed content model, which is explained in Chapter 6.

Figuring out what's a domain object and what's just an attribute can get tricky. There's no "correct" answer here. It depends on how you choose to represent your domain.

When you get stuck, ask yourself some questions:

Does this concept contain other useful and reusable concepts?

If so, it's probably a domain object. We describe our Session object using attributes such as Name, Description, Location, Host, Time, Date, and Time. We'll want to reuse this general form for every instance of a Session. Attributes can hold specific values (something like 3:30 p.m. or *Where Next for Empathy?*). You'll notice that some of the so-called attributes (like Host) are themselves domain objects. That's fine; a complete domain object (or "entity") can be an attribute of another object even if it has attributes of its own.

Can this concept be answered with a specific value?

If it can, then you're probably dealing with an attribute of a larger domain object. Attributes are things like Phone Number, URL, Description, Photo, Ingredient, and Top Speed. If you find yourself looking to include concepts like this, work backward. Figure out what they're attributes *of*. You may end up discovering a larger domain object.

Does this concept have specific relationships to existing domain objects?

If it does, it may be best to represent it as a domain object. Think about Session and Session Type. Remember that an example of a Session might be Board Game Evening with a session type of Social. So why have Session Type as a full domain object and not just an attribute of Session? On our project, we knew that different session types can behave a little differently. A sponsor might give us money to spend on all the social events. Workshops may have specific coordinators and specific price and availability attributes. So while Session Type is answered by a specific value, it was helpful to relate some things to *types* of session rather than to sessions themselves.

Is this concept expressed as an object in other domains?

One of the cool things about domain modeling is the ability to reuse objects in other models. If you modeled the subject Information Architecture, you can bet you'd reuse objects from the IA Summit conference domain. The Person and Topic objects connect the wider practice of IA with the things or people who shaped it. Should you find yourself modeling several domains, think about the objects you can share across them.

Does this concept need a specific representation in the interface?

In other words, if this were a website, would this thing need its own page? If so, then it's a domain object. You almost certainly want a specific representation for each Person and Session. That way, every session or speaker profile can be linked to, shared, or searched for. When you're likely to give something its own URL, make it a domain object.

Am I likely to want to expand on this concept in the future?

If so, you probably want to make it a domain object now. Today your tastes might be simple. Maybe you're modeling the domain Restaurants. You're thinking, "Hmm…I know I want Menu to be a domain object. Menus have items, so I'll define Menu Item as an attribute." Great start, and that might suit your needs just fine for today. But in the future, you may find that those unsung little menu items are the meat and potatoes of your restaurant business. They're your signature *dishes*—the stuff that people are perhaps most interested in. In that case, you'll want to whip up that Menu Item attribute into a full domain object: Dish, perhaps, with related attributes like Ingredient, Cuisine, or Diet. As always, think hard about what's most interesting. The menu is only the playlist. It's the stuff on the list that we care about.

Domain objects represent rich concepts that break down into attributes. Don't include attributes in the domain model. If they come up in group discussion, by all means capture those decisions for later. You'll be using them soon. But leaving them out of this model makes the diagram easier to read and less subject to change. It also helps keep your thinking at a high level. But hey, if some attributes end up expressed as full objects, it's not a problem. It may even signal some future requirements you've yet to explore.

FINDING A UBIQUITOUS LANGUAGE

As a team you're going to spend a long time referring to the same things. Meetings. Design and code reviews. Usability testing sessions. Over and over you'll talk about the same domain objects. You need a common vocabulary—what domain-driven designers call a *ubiquitous language.*

This is nothing more than agreement on how everything's named and defined, though agreement on language isn't always straightforward. Teams can lose sight of their audience and skew toward technical or domain-specific jargon. Terms should make sense to everyone on the team, but also to the domain experts and users. The names of domain objects and relationship values should come from your research.

If you're struggling to give something a clear name, it could be that your concept isn't well-defined. Once, when working on a model for a music service, we debated whether to name a concept "account" or "profile." It turns out we'd mangled a couple of concepts and our one domain object needed to be two.

Use consistent terms across database table names, CSS classes, and style guides. Your terms should be clear and self-explanatory enough to use even as navigation labels in your interface. Insist in meetings that everyone stick to the correct terms. It's not unusual for engineers to fall back to technical jargon that feels more familiar. But listen for terms that just refuse to stick. It might be that the term chosen doesn't reflect the concept it's meant to describe. In that case, revisit the model and make sure your original understanding still holds. It's fine to make changes—just make sure your model and your terms are in sync. A ubiquitous language helps keep your project team on the same page. If it isn't spoken, it isn't alive. Your goal is consistency through code, content, and user interface design. Make your ubiquitous language part of your everyday project conversation.

ESTABLISHING CARDINALITY

So far you've used a simple connecting line to show a relationship between two domain objects. Nothing simpler than good ol' boxes and arrows. But what if those relationships come with strings attached? Sooner or later you'll need to express some ground rules about how things connect.

Cardinality is counting how many of something can relate to something else. A car has only one engine. A person has at least one name but could have more. A dish has many ingredients. A musician may be part of zero, one, or many bands. That's cardinality at work. You express it using crow's foot notation (though other fine notation formats are available). Let's look at the three main types of relationships.

ONE-TO-ONE (1:1)

In a 1:1 relationship, one instance of one object relates to only one instance of another object. A specific key opens only a specific lock (**FIGURE 5.7**). And that specific lock can be opened only by a specific key. A specific Social Security number is assigned to a specific person. That person is assigned only that number. In practice, true one-to-one relationships are rare. If you encounter one, ask yourself whether both concepts are true domain objects. It may be that one is merely an attribute of the other.

FIGURE 5.7
A 1:1 relationship.

ONE-TO-MANY (1:*N*)

In a 1:*n* relationship, an instance of an object can relate to several instances of another object. A sports team has many players, but they all belong to only that team (**FIGURE 5.8**). A session has one venue, but that venue probably hosts several sessions. Charles Dickens wrote a bunch of great books, but each book was written only by Charles Dickens. *Great Expectations* was published in many different editions, but they're all editions of the same book. Charles Dickens kept many chickens, but each chicken had only one owner. One-to-many relationships are the most common type you'll encounter.

FIGURE 5.8
A 1:*n* relationship.

MANY-TO-MANY (*M:N*)

Is it getting crowded in here? In an *m:n* relationship, several instances of an object relate to several instances of another. At first glance, this might seem to happen all the time. Take that Book and Author example from before—some books (like this one) have more than one author. So it looks correct to say that several authors can write several books (**FIGURE 5.9**). But that becomes complicated. Your average relational database would have a meltdown. In fact, true many-to-many relationships are rare. If you find yourself faced with one, it's a reasonable bet that you're missing a domain object. This bit is important, so let's elaborate.

FIGURE 5.9
An *m:n* relationship.

On first inspection, it seems possible that `Author` to `Book` should be an *m:n* relationship (**FIGURE 5.10**).

An author can write one or more books.

A book can have one or more authors.

FIGURE 5.10
An *m:n* relationship.

For the model to inform the database design, you must resolve the *m:n* relationship into two 1:*n* relationships. You can do this by moving a few things around and creating a whole new domain object.

First, instead of `Author` as an object, try `Person`. After all, authorship alone doesn't define a person. And maybe you'll want to reuse a `Person` object from another domain.

Now create that new object. Call this the `Collaboration`. This object acts as a junction between `Person` and `Book` and defines the lineup of people (Strunk and White, Carrie and Mike, James Patterson and whoever…) who wrote a specific book. Now you can say:

One person can be part of one or more collaborations.

One collaboration can write one or more books.

And *voila!* The *m:n* becomes two 1:*n* relationships (**FIGURE 5.11**). Who knows, that `Collaboration` object could be valuable in itself. It's like the difference between shouting out a bunch of songs and defining a playlist.

FIGURE 5.11 Two
1:*n* relationships.

The catch here is that now a person has to be associated with a book via the collaboration, even when they're only collaborating with themselves. For that reason, maybe `Collaboration` isn't the best name, but we couldn't think of a better one. Can you?

OPTIONAL RELATIONSHIPS

Charles Dickens may have many pet chickens, but ironically, poor old Roald Dahl has no chickens at all. So a person may have zero, one, or more than one pet. In crow's foot, you can make a 1:1 or 1:*n* relationship optional by adding a circle to represent the zero (**FIGURE 5.12**).

FIGURE 5.12
Optional
relationships.

RECURSION

A recursive relationship connects a domain object to itself. Let's take a classic workplace example. One or more employees are managed by a manager. Simple enough, right?

But hold on, isn't that manager also managed by someone? And that someone is in turn managed by someone else? And really, is a manager a different class of person than an employee? (Hey, c'mon now. Be nice.) We could tidy this up by saying that an `Employee` manages zero, one, or many employees (**FIGURE 5.13**). It's a recursion all the way up to the head honcho on the 40th floor. And even she's an employee.

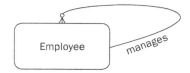

FIGURE 5.13
A recursive
relationship.

Don't take offense when you hear people refer to this notation as a "pig's ear." They're not critiquing your work.

Adding cardinality to a domain model is a pro move. It's fine detail and not something you'd always include in the first draft, but it provides the important business logic you'll soon need to move from paper to data.

KNOWING WHEN TO STOP

You know that time when you meant to tidy a few loose papers and before you know it you've cleaned the whole house? Yeah, us neither—but modeling can be like that. Knowledge is sprawling and unordered. It can be hard to focus on one piece without following the rabbit hole to anything and everything else.

CHUNK YOUR MODEL

One tactic is to assign ownership of parts of the model to different people on the team. It's a little like working on a jigsaw puzzle as a group, as each person builds out a subsection. This helps them focus on one part of the problem. Regroup often as a team to compare your pieces and make sure they fit together. Working this way builds peer review into the process and exposes differences in understanding. It's easier to update small parts of the model independently than to update the entire thing at once. Indeed, some parts may need more iteration than others. Just make sure you keep checking in as a team and sharing your progress.

FIND THE BOUNDARY OBJECTS

Often, you'll define an object that could also belong to different subject domains. Take Song from the earlier example of Live Music. That object could be equally at home in the domain Recorded Music. (Though is a live version of a song truly the same thing as the recorded version? Maybe you'd need to throw a Version or Performance object in there.) These are *boundary objects*, because they mark the gateway to adjacent domains. When you come across one, be careful to stay focused on your original domain. It's easy to wander off-course and start modeling out the entire universe.

Maintain distinct domain models for the different subjects you want to cover. That's so much easier to manage than a one-model-to-rule-them-all approach. Boundary objects are your magic portals from one subject to the next. The BBC once modeled out all the TV shows they broadcast, episode by episode—right down to the songs featured in the track list. A show such as *Mad Men* is full of cool 1960s music. The BBC's page for each episode listed every song heard, along with the original recording artist. In the underlying model, `Song` and `Artist` were boundary objects also used by the BBC Music service (with its own domain model). That made some magic possible. Bob Dylan's entry in the *Mad Men* tracklist linked automatically to the Bob Dylan page on BBC Music. By connecting `TV` to `Music` through boundary objects, they opened up new user journeys. People could look up a song they heard on TV and follow a tight connection to the heart of the artist and their music.

BRINGING IN EXPERTS

During your initial research, you made some new friends of the experts and enthusiasts. In an ideal world, you'd make them part of the modeling crew. They'd sit in on all your meetings and help you thrash it all out. In practice, this is rarely practical. So here's a couple of ways to make sure your modeling has an expert's seal of approval.

BRING EXPERTS IN EARLY

Domain modeling doesn't have to come *after* meeting with subject-matter experts and users. As mentioned in the last chapter, it's just as good (maybe even better) to start *sketching* the model while you have them. This can clarify the points they bring up in conversation; such is the power of visual thinking.

Collaboration works best while the model still looks rough. Sketches and sticky notes beat a slick diagram that's printed out or, worse, displayed on a computer screen. You have a bunch of boxes and arrows that may not have the right labels, may not be complete, and may need connecting. Make everything easy to erase or reposition. Modeling is messy. People engage more when they can get hands-on.

However you choose to involve them, schedule regular check-ins with your experts, users, and stakeholders. Anyone should be able to follow the model and so understand your take on the subject. It's a great conversation piece.

We've always found that when we get deep into modeling we start to see our subject as a series of interlocking parts. But don't assume that even an expert thinks in the same way. Their mental model is probably rooted in practical examples, not abstract concepts and relationships. Be ready to help them to think at a higher altitude.

BRING THE EXPERTS BACK

As you model, questions will come up, usually around the difference between two domain objects or the possible connections between them. Should you connect the `Chef` object to the `Dish` object? Or is it the `Recipe` object? Maybe both? This is the time to go back to the experts.

If your SMEs are also your project stakeholders, then it's double brownie points. You're bringing them into the design process, where their expertise is the most influential. It sure beats asking them to judge an art show of wireframes.

Ask your SMEs things such as:

Does this make sense?

This seems an obvious question to start with. We say that anyone should be able to read the model. Still, walk them through your thinking anyway. This time they'll be asking the questions, so listen for any points of confusion. You may yet need to get out the sticky notes and white-out while your experts are still in the room. Note any political differences of opinion, but try to keep these separate from an objective appraisal of your model's validity.

Are we using the right terms?

Research informs the names you choose for your domain objects. You've taken input from experts, from users, and from your own team and stakeholders. What you name your domain objects is then your call. You might have good reasons for deviating from an "official" term. (Often some expert terminology is too highfalutin for the folks back home.) Make your case to the experts. Get their blessing that even when your terms are different, they're not wrong.

Is this always true?

Remember that omnishambles when we called something `Hotel` when we really meant `Venue`? Man, dark days. Something we assumed to always be true turned out to have notable exceptions.

Since your model guides your design decisions, you want it to have a decent shelf life. Run through actual examples using specific instances of each domain object. Look for examples that suggest changes to either your domain objects or your relationships.

What's missing?

A model is an abstraction of reality. It's always going to be a little reductive. Sometimes a lot. Prioritize the most significant concepts—things without which the subject can't be fully understood. Simplification is a high-wire act, especially when you're not a subject-matter expert. Walk them through examples to confirm that the decisions you've made haven't broken the model. Then again, your expert may fixate on some arcane point of process that matters to no one but them. Try to get more than one expert opinion.

Missing objects may also signal disagreement about the domain you're attempting to model. What people call a "subject" is just an arbitrary lasso thrown around a subset of knowledge. People don't always agree on the boundaries.

WHO USES THE MODEL?

Together your team filled journals with interview notes. Your wastepaper basket brimmed with collective attempts to understand and sketch out relationships. You spent hours over pizza, debating what to call the things within your domain. How to define them. How they fit together. The team has soaked up enough domain knowledge that you could chat to a stranger in a bar and pass for experts yourselves. And to crown all that study, you arrived at a domain model so elegant and so simple (yet powerful) that any one of you could draw it on a whiteboard and discuss the finer details of your specialist subject. Go team!

Soon you'll all start to show your superpowers. Content design. Interface design. Database and CMS design. These steps should be collaborative too. But even when you can't work together, you'll always have the domain model. It's now your common reference point to guide each discipline.

Who will use this marvel and how?

INTERFACE DESIGN AND ENGINEERING

You're going to design and build the interfaces that connect people to content. These windows into the world represent the content resources first described as domain objects. Through interface design and navigation, you'll show how these resources fit together. Flip to Chapter 9, where we go deep on this.

BACK-END ENGINEERING

If you're a back-end engineer, we bet you'll see a domain model and start thinking of database tables. You're no stranger to entity relationship modeling. This looks pretty much like the process you'd go through anyway. You've been able to help your team see the world as objects and relationships. Most content management systems (whether off the shelf or home-grown) run from a relational database. Design this database to map to the research-validated model. More of that coming in Chapter 8.

CONTENT STRATEGY

For you folks working on the content itself, the domain model is a treasure map! It's a record of the kinds of content your general and expert audiences have told you they're interested in. You'll use it as reference to audit the content you have and make a plan for the content you need. Intrigued? Chapter 7 is your jam.

MORE EXAMPLES

Yeah, we know. Our IA Summit domain example may be helpful, but it's not the whole meatball. People ask us all the time for more examples to help cement the idea. Try these on for size:

THEME PARKS

Mike is crazy-obsessed with Disney theme parks. Modeling it made him think hard about what a theme park even is (**FIGURE 5.14**).

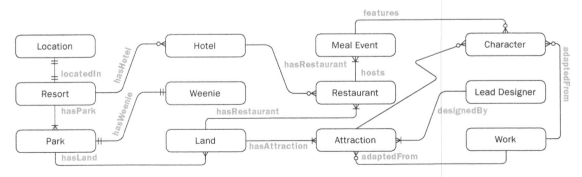

FIGURE 5.14 A theme park model.

Walt Disney World is a `Resort`, with a `Location` of Orlando, Florida.

Each resort has `Parks`, such as the Magic Kingdom or Epcot.

Each `Park` divides into `Lands` (Adventureland, Fantasyland). Each `Land` has `Attractions` (like Mike's favorite, the Haunted Mansion). There are also `Hotels`. These sometimes have a direct relationship to a `Park` (such as Animal Kingdom Lodge) and sometimes don't (Disney Pop Century).

Ooh, and each park also has a `Weenie`—Disney's term for a big piece of architecture used to help in wayfinding. In the Magic Kingdom, it's the castle. In Epcot, it's the big geodesic ball.

Each attraction has one lead designer (an Imagineer like Marty Sklar or Mary Blair). In practice, it would be difficult to credit everyone who worked on an attraction, so "lead" designer is sufficient. Also this avoids having to resolve the many-to-many relationship between designers and attractions. Attractions could be based on some prior creative work (as with Jules Verne's *20,000 Leagues Under the Sea*).

Each park has a `Restaurant` or six, as do the hotels. Each restaurant has `Meal Events` (Cinderella's Royal Table, anyone?), and those meals are usually associated with a specific `Character`. That character (we're looking at you, Pooh) may themselves be based on a prior creative work.

It's not a complex model (it's a small world after all) but one that tries to capture what's useful and interesting. It's reusable for any Disney resort and may even be suitable for any theme park anywhere.

> **NOTE** Disney sometimes calls their hotels "resorts," just to mess with us.

> **NOTE** Epcot's weenie is also an attraction, Spaceship Earth.

RESTAURANTS

From all the references to the BBC, you may well think our approach is only for big content publishers. What if you just want to make a website for your restaurant (**FIGURE 5.15**)? Let's give it a try.

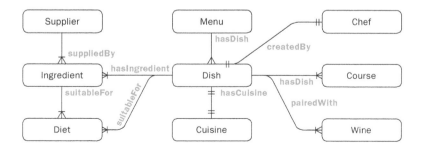

FIGURE 5.15
A restaurant model.

Every decent restaurant prides itself on the food. Each Dish is the plate of food served up (anything from lapsang souchong tea–smoked salmon to truffled mac-n-cheese).

Each Dish might be created by a particular Chef, adding a certain *je ne sais quoi* (usually to the price). A Dish gets served as a particular Course, so we know our starters from our desserts. And a Dish will likely have origins in a specific Cuisine (from French to Tex-Mex).

The Dish consists of Ingredients, important information for customers with food allergies. Speaking of which, Dishes may or may not be appropriate for a particular Diet (for example, kosher, halal, and celiac).

These days it's popular to list a Supplier to give the ingredients some provenance. It's not just a burger; it's a Happy Cow Farm grass-fed Angus burger.

We curate a set of Dishes (and courses) in a Menu. Choosing dishes for a menu is a fine art for the restaurateur. Many restaurants will have more than one menu available and may even rotate the menu daily.

Each dish on the menu could be paired with a Wine. Guess what—boundary object alert! Wine is of course a whole other domain that would be modeled separately and then linked to customers from the world of food to the broader world of wine.

Okay, admittedly this sounds like quite a fancy restaurant. And we've concentrated on the culinary aspect of the experience. But it pays to keep things focused on the concepts people find most delicious. Food for thought.

LIVE MUSIC

A favorite example of ours is the world of live music concerts (**FIGURE 5.16**), not least because it contains some unpredictability we can account for.

An Act is our term for either a solo artist or a group. If you or more likely your parents, have seen, Fleetwood Mac or the Drifters over the years, you know that "group" can be a fluid term. So for completeness' sake, perhaps you want to document the Lineup of a specific act.

This is the unpredictability we mentioned. An individual Performer is part of the Lineup rather than part of the Act. Take That are still Take That, regardless of whether Robbie Williams joins one night.

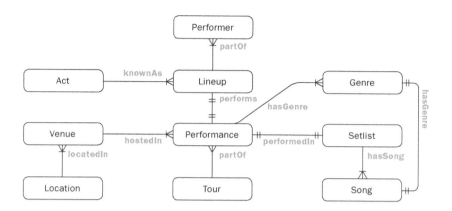

FIGURE 5.16
A music concert model.

A `Performance` is a single gig on a single date. Though maybe the hardest-working acts in show business give more than one performance each day.

Of course you care about each `Song` in the performance. (By the way, there's another possible boundary object.) But you also want to know which songs were in the `Setlist` for a given performance. Believe it or not, there are true fans out there who log this stuff.

A `Venue` (Madison Square Garden, Ronnie Scott's Jazz Club) holds a performance. Each performance can be part of a `Tour`, covering many venues across many `Locations`.

Finally, each performance, or an entire tour, could be in a certain `Genre`. Musical genre is another boundary object. It connects the gig to a bigger canvas of similar music, past and present. It also helps avoid Dylan's weird bluegrass stuff.

And you're done. She's a model, and she's looking good.

As with all these examples, take them and play with them. Run through examples. Look for any instances that would change how the model works. Add or remove objects and relationships until they work for you.

MODELING FOR THE FUTURE

The domain model maps the world of your chosen subject. It doesn't care which interfaces you'll build. It doesn't care what content you have. It models what your content will be about. Because as hard as it may be to swallow, no one cares about your content. They care about what they care about. Fine wine. Waterskiing. Himalayan travel. And all the points of interest within those topics. When you can map your content to those things, you stay focused on serving their needs. And then maybe they do start to care a little about your content, or at least recognize a kindred passion.

During your research, you'll definitely want to figure out underlying user needs and pain points. That's all in day's work for your average UX designer. But take the time to understand and respect the subject domain itself. That domain has its own structure, rules, and quirks. It shows everyone the real things that your audience cares about.

The model sets you up for the future. Use it to plan the content needed to serve the subject. Use it to uncover gaps in your inventory. Use it to determine which content makes the cut. Use it to guide the natural navigation of your product. Mapping content to concepts helps maintain structural integrity as your inventory scales. Whether you have a few dozen content resources or a few thousand, relationships between them remain the same. Don't feel pressured to represent the entire domain with content, at least not all at once. You're free to choose which parts of the model you'll expose in your interface designs. Remember, this isn't a site map.

Content changes often. Every good content strategist will tell you to keep it fresh. To a lesser degree, interfaces are subject to change. We update our visual identity. Change our layouts. Build whole new interfaces for emerging technology. But beneath all the content and UI lies the truth of what they represent. Of course, we can't claim that the domain itself never changes. New knowledge has increased our understanding of everything from astronomy to zoology. Yet as we dive from the surface of publishing and presentation to the depths of domain, change happens less.

Regardless of what you publish, or how often, follow the advice of your experts and users. Surface the meaningful relationships that give form to a subject. Everything you build is just a digital representation of something real. Understanding that reality should be where any design starts. Our content is just a means to someone's end.

Modeling—A Team Sport

AN INTERVIEW WITH MICHAEL SMETHURST

For more than a decade, Michael Smethurst has been one of the UK's most influential practitioners of domain modeling and structured content. A former BBC information architect, he writes extensively about web design and architecture at http://smethur.st. Michael now works within the complicated processes of UK Parliament, bringing sense and structure to parliamentary business information. We caught up with him to get a few tips about running modeling sessions.

What's the best way to run a domain modeling session?

Domain-driven design (DDD) is a team sport. It allows the whole team to immerse themselves in the gnarly details of the information space. We don't run them with any hard-and-fast rules. How we schedule a session largely depends on the culture and politics of the organization. Sometimes it's good to get people away from their normal work environment. We experiment with different locations to see what works best for conversation.

"Storytelling" might have become a design cliché, but stories and anecdotes are still the best vehicles for informal knowledge exchange. Our DDD sessions work best when we skip formality and get to a story as quickly as possible. We set up the room to avoid anything that could get in the way of conversation and informality. A whiteboard, some pens, and some chairs usually see us through. If we start sketching things out, it's important that the experts can see what we're doing and feel able to jump in when we're getting things wrong. If they grab the pen, so much the better.

Who should you invite to a session?

Make sure there are more of them than there are of you, but keep the group small. You want the domain experts to feel comfortable talking and explaining. That gets more difficult if they're attempting to explain to a roomful of people. I once sat through a session where the invite had been accidentally forwarded to a chunk of people from the computer department. We ended up with three domain experts and about ten assorted designers, developers, and user researchers. This was not good.

Almost everything else really depends on the culture of the organization. If it tends to be hierarchical, you probably need to look for people at roughly the same level. You don't want one person doing all the talking and everyone else feeling unable to chip in. If that happens, you'll never get

(continues)

(continued)

to free-flowing conversation and anecdotes. Some of the best sessions I've taken part in have come when people disagreed about how something works or how a particular situation has been dealt with in the past. Everyone in the room needs to feel comfortable enough to have these conversations.

A bridge person or translator can be handy. Someone the experts and stakeholders already know and trust who can help unlock details you might otherwise miss. If the organization has librarians or archivists or other people used to dealing with the information output of offices, grab one.

Finding the right people can be tricky and might involve trial and error. Most organizations have informal network structures. Take time to find these. Kitchen chats and corridor conversations can be routes to the right people. These are the places you find people you don't normally work with and who know a lot about your domain. Whoever you end up inviting, it's important not to handle the session too formally or look like you already know all the questions to ask. We don't write a script. We let the conversation flow and see where it goes. Occasionally we disappear down rabbit holes and need to nudge things back on track. These people are the experts. We're there to listen and to attempt to explain the things they've explained back to them. Until they smile.

There are no such things as dumb questions, even if some of them sound that way at first. But "dumb" questions often get the best answers. Be humble, show interest, show empathy, and never try to boss the session.

When is the best time to schedule a session?

The usual meeting etiquette applies. Don't aim for the end of the day, when everyone wants to go home. Don't start too early. People tend to have morning routines that they don't want disturbed. Never run over lunch. But do allow enough time. We've found that the first session with a new team can take a little while to find its balance. People often assume we arrived from the computer department to talk about computer things. Eventually they understand that we're not here to talk technology, we're here to talk about their job and their experiences. That's when the conversation opens up.

People like to talk about their work. They enjoy explaining their difficulties, and they don't often get the chance. I remember a trip to the House of Lords Private Bill Office. They spent the first 30 minutes misunderstanding why we were there and trying to figure out which software we wanted to talk about. But after patiently answering our dumb questions, they started to open up. After 45 minutes, the first minor disagreement happened. There was some debate about whether a certain thing had ever happened and what they'd done about it. Past 45 minutes, they forgot we were even there. Stories were told and anecdotes were given. If you get to this point, you've pretty much hit pay dirt. The difficult part is sketching quickly enough.

Finally, not all modeling happens in the room. People often realize they've forgotten something or misexplained. And the conversations continue, like with the person from the House of Commons Select Committee who followed me to the pub to complain about their information systems and how much additional effort was needed, due to poor design. That's when I realized the fundamental model we'd been designing with them didn't match their reality. No one had said anything in our previous meetings. But we'd managed to build enough trust and show this stakeholder enough interest to persuade her to explain her problems. We learned more during 10 minutes in the pub than we'd learned in a two-hour meeting. Informality helps communication.

CHAPTER 6

TRANSLATING TO A CONTENT MODEL

Now that your team has shown off how much they know about their area of expertise and created a domain model, they'll be excited about making it all come to life. Have patience! Some stakeholders—and even some of your team—may want to jump ahead. They're going to start talking about what will go on the website or how to build or design the product. But you aren't there yet. You still aren't talking about the CMS or any interface. You've got a little more work to do first.

CONTENT VS. EXPRESSION

The domain model provides the context. It grounds you in the real world, where users live and businesses operate. Content is the expression of paths through and between the objects of your domain.

You might think of the domain object as an atom. It's got a bunch of protons, electrons, and neutrons flying around inside it. It's time to look in the microscope and discover what those are. It's time for some structure. Enter the content model.

A content model represents the content and its relationships. It zooms in and provides structure to the objects that were mapped in the domain model. A *content type* is a reusable container for managing content by common structure and purpose. A *content model* is a visual representation of the content types in a subject area, their properties, and the relationships between them.

A content model is an evolution of a domain model and generally inherits the object names, providing a direct link between the models.

What we're suggesting might be a bit different from what you have seen in other content models, which usually are limited to a single website or product. We stick to the "boxes and arrows" approach for our content model. Keeping it in a simple visual format early allows non-technical stakeholders to stay involved at a point when their expertise is valuable—even essential. Don't worry! We'll get to a spreadsheet for each interface eventually. (How could we call ourselves content strategists otherwise?)

The content model should include content types for the specific area of your domain that matters to your business. Because the model focuses specifically on *your* business and audience, you might say that it focuses on the brand. For example, focus on the IA Summit specifically, not just any old conference. Or focus on Disney theme parks, not other theme parks, like Legoland or Dollywood. Be sure to keep the entire business in mind rather than a particular product. Staying away from a specific product will make your content portable and long-lasting.

FROM DOMAIN MODEL TO CONTENT MODEL

Getting from domain model to content model involves collaboration to harness the collective wisdom of your experts and users. Get ready for more sticky-note, whiteboard, brain-dump fun! Harry Potter fans might picture Dumbledore extracting his thoughts into the Pensieve for Harry to view. That's kind of what we're doing: getting thoughts from someone else's head (your experts and your team) and putting them into a form that others (your audience) can make sense of and use for their own benefit.

Where a domain model maps the world, a content model focuses on the structure and content you'll actually publish. Pick the objects and relationships from the domain model that make sense for your organization to address. You are part of a wider world. Claim your spot in it. The objects you expose from your domain model will depend on how you fit into the domain itself. If you modeled the right domain, though, you should be covering most of the objects in your content model.

When working on the IA Summit, we could have created a domain model that would be reusable for conferences generally or for ASIS&T conferences (the Association for Science Information & Technology, which runs the IA Summit), but we were concerned only with the IA Summit. We also could have considered the 2015 IA Summit specifically rather than all the events before and after. But we wanted to span the years and have a consistent and extensible repository for all the events. If we had gone with the more general `Conferences` domain model, we still could have limited our content model to the IA Summit. You're constantly evolving and making decisions about what spot to claim within the wider universe of your subject area.

DECIDING WHAT TO KEEP IN THE CONTENT MODEL

The first step is to put your domain model back on the board. You'll likely have some objects you might not want to include in the content model. Maybe they aren't part of your core business. Maybe you cannot speak to some concepts with authority. Or you might not have content for some of the objects yet. You can hide concepts from the domain model that you are not going to include in your content model. Remove, cross out, gray out, or otherwise hide the concepts and relationships that you will not be using.

Think twice about removing a connecting object. The lines are just as important as the boxes they connect, so pay attention to what happens to the lines when you hide an object. Do relationships change? If so, do the new ones still make sense? If they do, proceed. If not, document the decision that the object is needed to keep relationships intact.

What Objects Should be in the Content Model?

Here are some questions to guide your decision to keep or get rid of an object when going from domain model to content model.

Is it part of your core business?

If an object isn't something that matters to the success of your business, don't include it in the content model.

Do you have content for it?

Yes? Keep it in! No? Decide whether you'll create the content or leave that object off the content model for now.

Is it of interest to your audience?

If something is not of interest to your audience, why have content for it? (There are plenty of objects that experts want users to be interested in, but they simply are not.)

Does removing it fundamentally change a relationship?

Some objects serve the purpose of connecting other objects. Think carefully about whether removing it changes the way other objects are related or, indeed, removes the relationship (like Lineup in the Live Music example).

Will it increase your relevance to your audience?

Maybe an object is something that you don't have content for but that would give your SEO a boost or fill a gap that your audience craves. Or it will attract a new audience as you expand your brand. In those cases, it might be worth creating new content to form a better (or new) relationship with your audience.

Take the example of Live Music (**FIGURE 6.1**). A ticket seller probably doesn't need to worry about the Setlist or Song domain objects. It is tempting to remove Lineup. But Lineup connects Act and Performer. If you remove Lineup, you lose the ability to link an individual (Performer) who sometimes tours with a band (an Act). We see this often. A lead singer who normally tours with a band is on a solo tour. Or someone who is normally a solo act tours with a band—or put together a different band. Customers might search only for the most well-known part of that relationship. Keeping Lineup allows the connection to happen. You wouldn't want someone missing out because they searched for Neil Young, who might be touring with Crosby, Stills, and Nash this year. Or missing out on the Eddie Vedder ukulele tour because they searched for Pearl Jam. Or missing Elvis Costello, who is sometimes by himself, sometimes with the Attractions, and other times with the Imposters—three different acts.

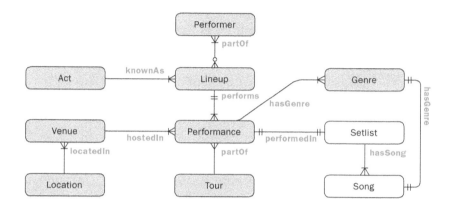

FIGURE 6.1 A ticket seller might not include the `Setlist` and Song objects in their content model.

COLLABORATING TO MAKE BETTER CHOICES

Because you've got everyone in your band back together, this is the time for your team to have conversations about what this model means for your organization. Any particular department or area may be responsible for only a subsection of the model. In that case, pay attention to the relationships and make sure all departments work together so that the content joins up. It does not matter who within the organization is responsible for concepts or whether some concepts might span many departments. Collaboration and high-level buy-in are essential to maintain objectivity and capture as much information as you can about your world.

In fact, this is part of the beauty of starting with the domain and then building a content model without worrying about an interface or product: You help create stakeholder alignment early. Everyone involved sees the connections and can account for them when it is time to create content. The benefits are potentially enormous. Less duplicate content, easier content curation, and more consistent customer experiences could be boons for your bottom line. But we're getting ahead of ourselves.

FROM OBJECTS TO CONTENT TYPES

At this point along the journey from abstract to specific, domain-model objects become content types with assigned attributes. Sometimes there isn't a straight line from a domain object (a real-world thing defined in the domain model) to a content type (a reusable container that describes the consistent form of similar content). You might find that what looked like a single concept is really two or three content types or that some objects get subsumed by others. New content types will emerge as objects come into focus. There is no "correct" answer. It's kind of a Goldilocks dilemma: finding just the right number of content types, not too many and not too few. You want as many as are useful for your team. You don't have to get it right the first time, either. You can add, remove, or change them at any time. Focus on what content you intend to support, and you'll keep going in the right direction.

MAKING GOOD CONTENT TYPES

When you know which parts of the domain model you are going to include as content types, you can start describing them. While you can think about how this will play out in the CMS, do your best to keep your thinking high level and not specific to any system.

In the wider world, a `Person` has many more attributes than are shown here (**FIGURE 6.2**). But in our `IA Summit` domain, we limited the set of attributes to what mattered to us. Does this include more or less than you thought? In our case, we thought outside the box of a single website but not so far that we included more than what conference attendees look for. We are thinking of a `Person` as a resource, a thing that can be used in many contexts as it relates to a conference—or even to many conferences. This broadens our perspective from thinking only about a website—or even about a specific instance of a conference. We wanted all these people to write blog posts, to show up on Lanyrd.com (a social conference directory), and to play multiple roles from year to year.

Considering the entire business case becomes even more important if you produce many conferences. You could reuse `Person` across the conferences and years. Carrie has participated in several of one organization's conferences over many years, as a participant and as a speaker. She's always the same person for each of those conferences, even when she's changed her name and title. Shouldn't the organization be able to assign her to any conference for any year rather than re-collect and re-enter all her information each time for each conference website? Name changes, job changes, photos, and bios could be updated once and spread across the instances.

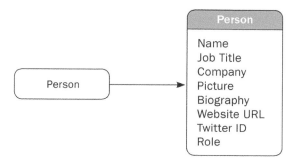

FIGURE 6.2 In the content model, you add attributes to a domain-model object to make it a content type.

Or maybe you don't want that information updated everywhere. That is a choice to make and a decision point. Modeling exposes complexity early in a project. Have the discussion now about what to do. In this case, ask

- Do we want the biographical information (title, company, biography text) to be tied to the person or to the event?

- Do we want each event to reflect the most current information or to reflect what was accurate at the time of the event?

Maybe it is important that a speaker's title and company for the 2014 event be whatever it was in 2014 while the information for the 2017 event is whatever was current in 2017. Now is the time to make this decision. It affects your model, and it will affect how you build your system. This and other decisions have to do with business rules rather than engineering. Don't leave it for engineers to decide. You will save untold hours of work later by dealing with the complexity up front.

DEFINING ATTRIBUTES

Everything has attributes. A car could be a red SUV with seating for five, a moonroof, a 4-cylinder/2.5L engine, a black interior, and a Bose stereo system. Or it could be a blue coupe with seating for four, a 4-cylinder/1.6L engine, a tan interior, and a Harman Kardon stereo system. When you buy a car, you care a lot about its attributes even if you think of them as "features" or "specifications."

NOTE We use the term *attributes* in this book, but in other places, you might see *properties*. We view the terms as interchangeable.

An *attribute* is a characteristic or quality of an object. Defining the attributes of your content types is the essence of the content model. Which ones you care about depend on your situation. When you're car shopping, price is probably a top attribute, as are color and reliability rating. If your family is growing, seating capacity and safety rating become important. When you walk up to a new car in a dealer's parking lot, you see a piece of paper in the window with these things and more listed. Open *Consumer Reports* and you'll see some of the same attributes, plus more.

Determining the Range of Attributes

When you think about objects as resources rather than as specific displays of information, you gain perspective that allows them to be platform neutral and thus reused, remixed, and restyled in many ways.

Take the example of a song. Looking at it from the highest level, it has dozens of attributes, including title, artist, songwriter(s), version, producer, length, recording date, genre, and more. You need to consider the use cases in your context to determine the range of attributes. If you thought only about the properties of a song for a TV show soundtrack, you'd use a different subset of the attributes than if you had a music streaming service. And in that streaming service, your mobile app would display different attributes in different styles than would the desktop app or the browser-based app.

Even considering multiple views of the content type itself within a single interface shows why a content resource should contain all its attributes. Each representation may contain only a subset of those properties. For example, a track listing for an album would list title, length, and version (if applicable). However, the detail display of the track would list title, length, songwriter(s), album, genre, and year recorded. If you thought only about the album listing, you'd have missed a lot of attributes.

Thinking in terms of a resource influences your definition of its attributes, making the content type scalable and flexible for use across systems and displays. And so, when you create a resource, all links can point back to that item rather than repeating the same content in multiple places or in various systems.

The British card game Top Trumps is based on comparing attributes of similar things. The topics are very wide ranging, from Sports Cars to Creatures of the Deep, and they come in special editions like Queen's Jubilee Celebration and

2012 Summer Olympics. To play, you choose from one of your cards an attribute that you think is better than the other players' attributes, and you call out the attribute and its value. Whichever player has the best value for that attribute gets to keep the cards. Play continues until one player has all the cards. Oh, the hours of entertainment people get from comparing things!

But we digress. The point is that the manufacturer has made a game from comparing four or five attributes of things. And it's a perfect illustration for a content type. The Sports Cars deck (**FIGURE 6.3**) describes the car in two sentences and breaks out certain attributes:

▪ Top speed (MPH)

▪ Engine size

▪ Cool factor

▪ Innovation

▪ Year launched

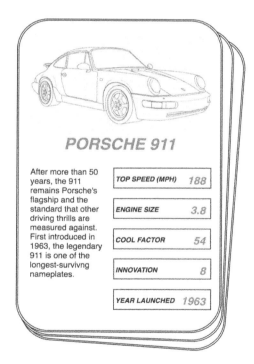

FIGURE 6.3 Top Trumps players compare the attributes of specific examples of a type of thing, such as a sports car.

Of course, there are many more attributes for each car, but these five were the ones the creators chose as most interesting to game players. In a roomful of automotive engineers, the list of attributes would expand greatly. If we were lucky enough to get an audience with John Lasseter and his *Cars* animators, we'd have a different set.

The context for defining attributes matters. You determined your context when you decided which subject domain to model. As you approach each content type, think about what attributes matter. Go to the edges of the world you know and maybe a step or two beyond. Think about how you might connect to other domains and which attributes would be needed to connect with them. You want to be prepared for the future. It is better to have too many attributes than not enough. If we thought we might want to have our IA Summit `Person` link up with the registration system, we would have included address, phone number, and email address as attributes so that we would be ready to make the connection.

With your group of experts and stakeholders, expand your domain object boxes to content type cards. You are getting in deep now. When the discussion moves from concept definitions to attributes, you start finding gaps, redundancies, and objects that don't need to be part of the content model. You may find that what you thought was a separate concept is really an attribute of something else.

In our `IA Summit` domain model, we decided that `Hotel`, while certainly an object and an entity in general, was not something that we needed to create content for or needed a URL specific to the IA Summit. For our purposes, it would be enough to include hotel information in the `Event` content type and link to the hotel's reservation system in the content itself.

COMBINING MULTIPLE OBJECTS INTO A SINGLE CONTENT TYPE

When we considered `Session`, `Session Format`, `Topic`, and `Track` objects, we spent time considering whether we needed entities for each of them (**FIGURE 6.4**).

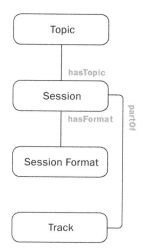

FIGURE 6.4
Subsection of the
IA Summit domain
model related to
Session.

You have many things to consider when it comes to deciding whether or not to combine objects in the content model. Here are some questions that will help you make the best decision for your situation (there are no right answers):

Will this object ever be displayed on its own as an entity?

One test is to think about how a concept will be represented in an interface or whether it will get its own URL. If it does, it is a resource and needs to be modeled appropriately as a domain object and a content type.

Likewise, if you want users to be able to navigate directly to the content or share a link in another context (like social media or email or just a user copying and pasting the URL somewhere else), it should be a separate content type. If it is shown only as part of another entity, it doesn't need to be a content type.

Does this object have more than one attribute?

Having only one attribute doesn't rule out an object becoming a content type, but think hard about why you'd keep it on its own. One reason is that it is part of a taxonomy scheme and you might want to be able to filter and sort by this entity.

How specific is the definition of the object?

> If the definition is so limited that it applies to only one instance of a content type, it probably does not need to be a content type. It's really useful only if it's reusable. In our IA Summit example, the Brand domain object was limited to a single instance—the IA Summit—and so wasn't a viable content type for our content model. Conversely, if you have an object with a single instance, you could expand the definition of the object to include multiple uses and have the need for the content type in your model.

Session
Session Title
Person
Description
Takeaways
Session Type
Topic
Time/Date
Duration
Venue
Room
Cost
Sponsor

FIGURE 6.5
Session content type.

After discussing these questions as a team, we decided that we would not use Session Format and Topic on their own. So we simplified our model by making them attributes of Session, not entities in and of themselves. As for Track, we decided it was not applicable enough to become part of the content model, so we excluded it. Four objects became one content type named Session (FIGURE 6.5).

We could have decided to keep Topic separate as an entity. But we envisioned Topic to be displayed only in the context of a session, so we didn't need it to be anything more than an attribute. If we wanted to have a topic page that would show a collection of all the content tagged with that topic (thus being a resource with a URL), we would have made a Topic content type.

Similarly, we considered Location. We had defined it as "Place the event is held. Different city each year." Did that need to be a content type? As defined, it would have only a single attribute and be related to an Event in a one-to-one relationship (so far, the Event has not been in the same city twice, and we did not anticipate that changing) (FIGURE 6.6). Many of the other objects contained a specific aspect of a location too. The concept Location had been too explicitly defined. Instead, several objects included some sort of location as an attribute (FIGURES 6.7 and 6.8).

As you can see, a lot of detailed thinking is involved in this step. You need to retain the context of your domain model while thinking specifically about how you will apply it in order to determine the attributes. Don't worry if your domain model feels simplistic and out of date now. You can always update it based on this new information.

Event
Name
Theme
Venue
Date
Duration
City
State/Province

FIGURE 6.6 Each `Event` is held in a `City` and a `State` (in the U.S.) or `Province` (in Canada).

Venue
Venue Name
Address
City
State/Province
Country
Geolocation
Telephone
Website URL

FIGURE 6.7 There are many `Location` attributes for a `Venue`, not just city and state, as with `Event`.

Session
Session Title
Person
Description
Takeaways
Session Type
Topic
Time/Date
Duration
Venue
Room
Cost
Sponsor

FIGURE 6.8 For a `Session`, the overall `Location` is linked through the `Venue` and also has a specific `Room` location.

ADDING TO THE MODEL

In our initial IA Summit model, we focused first on getting everything just right for the complicated content types, like `Session` and `Person`. Eventually, we realized we needed to model a `Blog Post` too. It could be considered an object (person – writes – post), and it had critical relationships with other content types in the model. A `Blog Post` (**FIGURE 6.9**) needed an author, which was really a `Person`, so was that another `Role`? And would it be related to the `Event` or the `Brand`? The decisions were documented in the content type.

Blog Post
Blog Title
Author
Body
Date
Topic
Event

FIGURE 6.9 The `Blog Post` content type we added to the IA Summit model after the domain-model objects were turned into content types.

Some things that aren't specific content types or objects will show up on your website or in your product. These will not be included in the model. They are things like the About page or your code of conduct. This is not the time to think about the entire inventory of content you'll end up with. It is the time to consider how to model the reality of the world and what things and connections your users want. Don't drive yourself crazy trying to get everything in the model. It will continue to evolve, and you can always come back and update it later.

RECONNECTING TO FORM THE CONTENT MODEL

You dissected everything to create your content types. You incorporated multiple objects into single content types, separated other objects into multiple content types, and added any new ones you discovered. Now you need to put it all back together again.

Relationships can be much more specific in the content model than in the domain model. Content types can be connected by linking attributes themselves rather than generally between the objects. Some attributes are entities themselves, and thus there are natural relationships between some content types. That is sometimes called an *entity reference*, because you are referring to another entity as an attribute, which creates a relationship.

Whether consciously decided or not, some of the content types' attributes are the same. And thus, the two content types become inherently connected. One example in our IA Summit model (**FIGURE 6.10**) is Topic, which is an attribute

FIGURE 6.10 Final IA Summit content model.

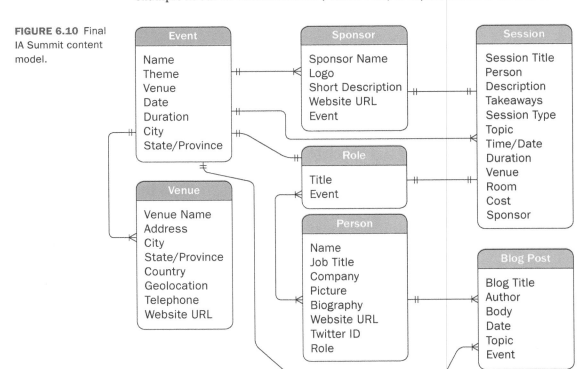

in both `Session` and `Blog Post`. Although we would not necessarily have connected those two content types, because they have that attribute in common, we can form a relationship that could enhance publishing in ways that will allow future Summit co-chairs to curate content in many ways.

Adding the relationships provides a richer palette with which to work and may even cause you to add some attributes. This is because you get granular enough that you discover new possibilities. Check your model by considering the original relationship from the domain model. Have you created attributes that allow the connection? Has the connection changed deliberately?

From our original domain model, with 12 objects, we ended up with seven content types (including the new one we added). We described the decisions around this evolution throughout this chapter. In summary, this is what happened to the six objects that didn't make the cut as content types:

- `Brand`, having just a single instance, became unnecessary.

- `Location` turned out to have multiple representations, depending on the content type, so it became an attribute of several content types.

- `Session Format`, `Topic`, and `Track` were really data about a `Session` and so became three of its attributes.

- `Hotel` was a boundary object and did not warrant us creating the content type or data relationship in our content model.

These were the choices we made for our use case. They are not necessarily the "right" choices for everyone. A different set of people modeling a different conference could have made different decisions and still ended up with a perfectly good model. Even another team working on the IA Summit could have put the model together differently. As long as you are making informed, collaborative decisions, you'll end up with a useful model that reflects your business rules, scope, and resources.

HOW THE CONTENT MODEL IS USED

There you have it: a visual representation of the types of content you have, their attributes, and connections. The content model does not consist of CMS requirements, but it will certainly be used as a basis for creating them. (Don't worry; we'll show you how to do that later.) It isn't a site map, but it is a guide for creating one—and it's a heck of a lot better than categorizing your content by format and making that your navigation menu. Although you didn't design an interface, you've thought about the parameters of all the ones you could create. You've deliberately staked a claim in your subject area by deciding what matters to your audience and to your business.

With the thinking you've done, you are in a position to create richer connections in the websites and products you'll create and to more creatively curate your content. On top of that, you've kept stakeholders involved in the design process in a meaningful way without asking them what features or functionality they want on the website or in a product. You've also had discussions that involved designers, developers, and content creators, and now they understand the basis for the interfaces they design, the systems they will build, and the content they will create.

We'd like to say that the human relationships you've developed during this process are invaluable, but there is a price tag on just about everything in a business. And you might have made the overall price for your digital presence a bit *lower* by making mistakes and redoing things when it is cheap and when a change can be made in the time it takes to erase or write a word on a whiteboard. Without the modeling, issues are often not uncovered until code is being tested or reams of content have been written. No one wants to redo anything after the budget is spent and time is up.

Much as an architect or a car designer creates a model before building the real thing, referring to it often, you have built a model before creating a digital product. When it's time to create a new product, enhance an existing one, or decide to retire one, you and your team should refer to your model to remind yourself of what is possible and advisable. Remix, restyle, and reuse your content, wherever it needs to go, by picking and choosing from the same set of criteria. With a complete content model—not just one for a single product—you can develop multiple representations of the same content across channels and systems.

How One Non-Profit Used a Content Model

AN INTERVIEW WITH JOSH TONG

Josh Tong is a content strategist at IREX, an international non-profit specializing in international education and development. In his role, he helps ensure that digital content can scale, be more efficient, reduce risk, and support the mission. In this interview, Josh shares his experience creating and using a content model during a recent website redesign project.

Why did you decide to create a content model for your website?

I thought it would help us ensure that we're building a better website, one that would be easier to both build and maintain.

Was it difficult to convince others of the need for a model?

Because introducing the idea of a model can confuse or overwhelm people, I incorporated *aspects* of the modeling process into the project and met people where they were. I started by creating templates based on what I heard from stakeholders and users. From there I worked through the content design, workflow, and business rules. When you add all those up, you end up with a content model plus direction for content creation, design, and the CMS build. We also kept a spreadsheet while working on this with stakeholders and developers. That helped keep everyone on track.

Does the content model have uses beyond the website?

Right now, it's just the website. But we have plans for extending it. In the short term, it has helped reset expectations about content types. We have really distinct content types for the new website. When they aren't distinct or built into the system, you end up with blobs. It will be useful when creating offline documents because there is a clear direction for what is needed.

In the longer term, there are opportunities to consolidate a lot of our websites and social media accounts (we have about 120 of those, combined). Even though some of our projects are required to have their own websites based on the terms of an agreement, we'll be able to map those new sites to the content model as a basis for creating them. And we'll be able to create them with a lower level of investment.

How did the content model help in the redesign project?

Our agency partner had a set process, so we didn't want to blow that up. Instead we made sure we were identifying content types early on. That was

(continues)

(continued)

part of the conversation in the discovery process. We were also able to use real content in wireframes. When designs had gray rectangles and no content, we could ask smart questions like, "What content type goes there?" "What happens when you click this link?" It was a way to design and review wireframes and build the CMS to make sure purpose and functionality were clear.

Our old system had several content types with structure, but we had lots of complaints about too much structure. Authors felt locked in to a format that didn't serve the organization. So we needed to figure out the right pieces and how to build things modularly while maintaining some flexibility without dumping everything in the body field.

How long has it been since you launched your website? What has been different in the time since then compared to websites you've worked on that were not based on a model?

It's been a year now, and it's gone well. We've got distinct content types that have held up. It's been a learning process for everyone involved, but people have embraced it. We need to make sure we're really using the model and not just using a placeholder for something. It's been easier to build out components because there is a real user need and a business need involved. Because we have a modular system, it's easier to create content.

It's easier to maintain. There is much less ambiguity about what content is needed than previously. Our taxonomy has evolved organically after doing a crosswalk and mapping to a short list to create a single taxonomy, which helps automate things.

What would you do differently if you were to do it again?

Not much. The project went smoothly and stayed on schedule. We did increase the budget from the initial projection, but that was based on a deliberate decision to add templates.

With more time, I would start with a domain model and map our metadata to Schema.org to let us include structured metadata in our pages. We need to make sure we can continue to evolve beyond the screen, and we're prepared to take that next step.

We also haven't done true COPE (create once, publish everywhere), since this is just one website. We're looking at opportunities to extend or create new content models for satellite sites. But we don't want to get ahead of ourselves. We do have budgeting and staff constraints. We are being deliberate and conservative so we can stay the course.

PUBLISHING CONTENT

CHAPTER 7

DESIGNING CONNECTED CONTENT

We know, we know. You bought a book about content design, and so far we've talked only about research and structure! But the trick to designing connected content is planning those connections in advance. Digging those solid foundations before building upward. Making sure you're in the right problem space before spending time and money on solutions. That planning pays dividends. Structure, first suggested by research and then expressed through domain and content models, provides a plan for your content work. It ensures that the content you create is rooted in the right domain territory. Your product is your digital property. Think location, location, location.

So now let's talk about the content itself. After all, it's the reason visitors come to your website or open your app in the first place. They're coming with specific goals in mind. Once you understand those goals, you can meet them through the content you provide—content specifically designed to match their mental model.

UX FOR CONTENT

Once upon a time, "going online" felt like traveling to another dimension. The screech of a modem signaled your arrival, and from there on you were pretty much on your own. A long, slow hunt for information through pages that took forever to load.

Back then, long-form text content was everywhere. The web took its cues from print publishing, with its metaphors of pages, headlines, and body copy. (Even today, that notion of a "page" as a unit of content is hard to shake.) You'd hear phrases like "content is king" and "if you build it, they will come." Many businesses interpreted this as a "more is more" strategy. Filing cabinets full of multipage documents and PDFs emptied out onto the internet. Here's everything! You go right ahead and figure out what's useful to you!

Times have changed. In the past few years, content strategists have shone a spotlight on the need for content that efficiently meets the information-seeking needs of known audiences. Content that focuses only on what's useful and presents a structure that helps build understanding, in other words, content that is explicitly *designed*.

Content design follows the broader principles of user experience (UX) design. UX designers start their process by figuring out who their audience is and what those people need most. Next, they explore possible solutions to meet those needs. And through a cycle of feedback and learning, they refine a solution until the original goals are met.

UX design considers an entire experience, in which content plays a pivotal part. However, many designers direct their efforts to improving the efficiency of the interface rather than critically evaluating the content itself. This is where you come in. As the content specialist, you make sure the content is well structured, focused, and appropriate to the audience. We could write a whole book on what makes content well designed, but the content strategist Sarah Richards does it so much better in her book *Content Design*. That said, we offer some general principles to consider:

- **Well-designed content is useful.** Bottom line, job one. Content doesn't sit there to look pretty. It has a job to do. No one comes to your website to hang out. They aren't taking time out of their day to "experience" your "brand story." They're coming to get stuff done. Whether your content is there to inform, educate, inspire, or even entertain, it has a goal to meet.

- **Well-designed content is usable.** It not only provides the information people need but makes that information easy to access, understand, and act upon. It has audience-appropriate terminology and literacy level, clear and consistent formatting and presentation, and support for different devices. How often have you felt the pain of trying to find and read a restaurant menu online, awkwardly pinching and zooming around a PDF? Good usability design isn't only for interfaces. It's needed for the content itself.

- **Well-designed content is findable.** Content that people can't find is no better than content you didn't write. Being findable means that it's available in open formats (such as HTML) and is crawlable by search engines. It means adding metadata that describes to those engines what your content is about. It means that it's housed within well-designed information architecture so that when people visit your product, they can navigate efficiently toward their destination. And above all, it means creating content that maps to the things people look for.

- **Well-designed content is focused.** No one ever curled up in their comfiest armchair, poured a glass of wine, and lost themselves in a good website. We all want to get in, grab the information we're looking for, and get the hell out. People are busy and distracted. They're half-reading your content on their phone as they walk to work. Life's too short for meandering content. TL;DR (too long; didn't read), as they say. Well-designed content stays on topic. As short as it needs to be, but no shorter. It puts the most important information first. Each piece is self-contained, making sense even when read out of sequence.

- **Well-designed content is targeted.** In UX design, there's a common axiom: "You are not your user." It's a reminder that the people we make things for have different needs and perspectives than we do. Different areas of interest and questions to ask. A set of animal videos aimed at kids would be very different than a collection aimed at zoologists. The reason you base content design on user and domain research is to figure out the most pressing things for your target audience.

- **Well-designed content is distinctive.** Whatever your topic, you're not the first to write about it. When you publish your content to the web, you're contributing to a wider conversation. What's your point of view? How is your take different from, or more valuable than, what's already out there? When people look for information, they don't immediately seek out one source and close the door on all the others. They "pogo stick" between a set of search results and the destination pages listed. Back and forth, they scan and skim-read, hunting for answers until they find a good enough solution. When they land on your content, what will make them stop and take notice?

■ **Well-designed content is connected.** As designer Charles Eames remarked, "Eventually everything connects." The pursuit of knowledge is a never-ending journey. Understanding of a subject comes not only from the content but also from the context. The way each piece of content links to another helps us understand how concepts relate. Create links between your pieces of content. And when your content inventory doesn't hold all the answers, link to the content of others. Cross-referencing information from many sources is what the world wide web was designed to do.

Designing effective content is challenging, but the work you've done so far has set you up for success. You've researched what experts consider authoritative. You sense-checked this against what your audience has told you they want to see. And you designed models that define how those things are connected. Time to fill in the blanks.

CONSTRUCTING CONTENT RESOURCES

Beyond the broad goal of creating content to meet audience needs, you'll come across different schools of thought around content design. Our process is rooted in structure, stemming from the objects you first defined in your domain model and then refined in your content model. Each of those objects describes a generalized type of thing—a conference session, a theme park attraction, a concert performance—right down to the common attributes that describe it.

Your aim is to provide content for each *instance* of every object in your model. Content for each specific conference session, each specific theme park attraction, and each specific concert performance. That content serves as an authoritative *resource* for the topic in question—a kind of digital stand-in for the thing itself.

That resource can be represented in many ways, such as a web page, an app view, or even a part of your printed brochures. Each resource can fuel many representations at once and later support the representations you haven't even thought about designing yet. For that reason, we design our content resources before designing interface representations.

User-Centered Content: A Lesson from History

In 1931, Indian librarian Siyali Ramamrita Ranganathan transformed how we think about accessing information. His "five laws of library science" were a radical departure from established practice. Even today, they have a lot to teach us about great content design.

First law: Books are for use

Of course they are, but libraries at the time often kept books in literal chains for storage and preservation, but not for use. Without access to the books, what's the point of having them? Focusing on use demands attention to the whole environment. Both the content and our ways of retrieving it must provide a rewarding experience.

Second law: A book for every reader

If books are for use, then the books available should address the requirements of each reader. Give everyone access to the materials they need. Expert curation connects the right content to the right person.

Third law: A reader for every book

If you're stocking a library, where do you prioritize? Where do you stop? Focus on what's needed, and cut out what isn't. No matter how much space you have, there's no sense in filling it with stuff no one ever reads.

Fourth law: Save the reader's time

Through sensible classification and cross-referencing, make information easy to find wherever people are. Design access to be fast and efficient.

Fifth law: The library must grow

It's a living organism. It must scale without breaking. It must continue to measure its own relevance. It must evolve to stay relevant.

S.R. Ranganathan recognized that access to useful information is a conscious design decision. A commitment to careful curation. Content needs to be designed to meet the needs of its readers. Your content might be about your business, but it's not for your business. It's not a personal fanzine. It's not a mouthpiece for your CEO to speak their brains to the world. Like books, content is for use. As Ranganathan said, you need a reader for every book. You're the custodian of one small section of the biggest library the world has ever known. Time to lay down the law.

AN ODE TO WIKIPEDIA

Hands up if you use Wikipedia. We thought so. As we write this, Wikipedia is the fifth most popular site on the internet. There are many great things about Wikipedia, but one thing in particular makes it an invaluable reference guide. Each article covers exactly one topic. One topic, one page. And there's one URL to locate it.

Want to brief friends on the rules of blackjack? Fire up your instant messenger app and paste a link to https://en.wikipedia.org/wiki/Blackjack.

Want to reference Anne Hathaway, the wife of William Shakespeare rather than the movie actor? https://en.wikipedia.org/wiki/Anne_Hathaway_(wife_of_Shakespeare)

Want to marvel at how detail-oriented the Wikipedia community can be? https://en.wikipedia.org/wiki/Toilet_paper_orientation

Whatever the topic, there's a crisply defined article of reasonable quality. Some may question the true authority of these articles. But to quote its own strapline, Wikipedia is a "free encyclopedia that anyone can edit." Don't agree with an article? You're free to improve it. The single-topic focus makes it easy to know what you should and shouldn't be writing about. And should your article start to drift in focus, the vigilant editor community won't hesitate to split it into several distinct, interlinked pieces.

It's the generous hyperlinking between articles that defines the Wikipedia experience. We've probably all had an endless stream-of-consciousness journey across Wikipedia articles. This kind of browsing is intentional and very different from a frustrating needle-in-a-haystack information hunt in a poorly structured product. There's real joy in jumping from one topic to the next as we explore the tributaries of knowledge itself.

Wikipedia is crowdsourced—more than 40 million articles in over 290 languages. Even the Wikimedia Foundation's 280 employees couldn't crank out that much work. Their one-topic-per-article approach is the only practical way this kind of distributed content management could work at scale. Every article is independent. Editors add links and metadata tags to stitch each part into the encyclopedic whole.

ONE TOPIC PER RESOURCE

So why the love letter to Wikipedia? (Aside from the fact that it's one of the most valuable resources we have. Donate them the price of a latte the next time they ask.)

It's because your content resources should use the same approach: each one strongly focused on a single topic. That topic is a specific instance of its content type. Remember in Chapter 5 when we looked at sports cars in the card game Top Trumps? Let's say your content model included a content type called Vehicle because research had shown that information on specific vehicles was what your petrol-head audience wanted to see. Each resource you published would focus solely on one topic—one specific vehicle. One on the Ferrari F355, one for the Porsche 911, and so on. Your Porsche 911 resource is your definitive destination for everything you want to say about that car. If someone were to ask "what's the Porsche 911 all about?" you wouldn't hesitate to point them in the direction of that resource.

What will that resource tell you about the car? Here, too, your previous research and modeling work pays off. In the Vehicle content type, you've defined a number of attributes. These now serve as the outline for your Porsche 911 resource, and indeed for every other resource of the Vehicle type (**TABLE 7.1**).

TABLE 7.1 **ATTRIBUTES OF A** Vehicle **CONTENT TYPE**

ATTRIBUTE	EXAMPLE CONTENT
Name	911
Manufacturer	Porsche AG
Description	The Porsche 911 is one of the most powerful sports cars made since 1963. It has a rear-mounted six-cylinder boxer engine and all-round independent suspension. It has undergone continuous development, though the basic concept has remained little changed.
Designer	Ferdinand Alexander Porsche
Photo	911.jpg
Video	911_in_torino.mp4

(continues)

TABLE 7.1 **ATTRIBUTES OF A** Vehicle **CONTENT TYPE** *(continued)*

ATTRIBUTE	EXAMPLE CONTENT
Year Introduced	1963
Body Style	2-door coupe
Engine Layout	Rear engine
Related Models	Carrera RS, 911SC

Each of these attributes should be supported by content. In some cases (such as Name), that content is simply a string of text denoting the car's name. In other cases (such as Description or Video), your content could offer much more detail, such as a feature-length article or multiple descriptive videos. Should you need to, adding extra attributes (such as History or Sales Figures) would give that longer content even more structure, providing you with more layout options later.

Think of the attributes as components of the resource, each of which can hold as much content as you need in order to meet your audience goals. Taken as a whole, the content type is in effect a well-defined structure for authors to build a resource for each topic.

ONE RESOURCE PER TOPIC

As Wikipedia does, publish just one principal resource to serve as a definitive guide. It serves as a common reference point, defining and disambiguating a concept. It's something to point to whenever you want to refer to the Porsche 911.

Depending on your needs, you might then continue to publish a separate resource for Ferdinand Alexander Porsche, one for the company Porsche AG, perhaps even one to explain the concept of rear-engine design. In fact, that's what Wikipedia already does:

- https://en.wikipedia.org/wiki/Porsche_911

- https://en.wikipedia.org/wiki/Ferdinand_Alexander_Porsche

- https://en.wikipedia.org/wiki/Porsche

- https://en.wikipedia.org/wiki/Rear-engine_design

One Resource per Topic? Really?

Limiting yourself to one resource per topic isn't as proscriptive as it may sound. Let's say you wanted to publish (or link to) some reviews for the Porsche 911. Wouldn't this mean publishing more than one resource that refers to the same thing? Yes and no. It's true that each review is about a specific car, but they don't serve to *represent* that car. Rather, your `Vehicle` content type would include an association to a separate `Review` content type. This would make clear the distinction between the car itself and reviews about it. It's similar to how we associated a `Blog Post` with a `Person` in the `IA Summit` domain. Each blog post is written by a person, but the blog post is not the same thing as the resource that represents that person.

Each resource represents a real concept connected by real-world relationships already defined in your model. Those resources can be rich in valuable text, photo, audio, and video while maintaining focus on a single topic.

Maintaining single-topic resources helps you make sense of your content. The approach has several advantages:

- **Keeps content focused.** Forcing each resource to specialize on a narrow topic helps you stay relevant to the reader's interest. People looking to explore further can follow your links to related content.

- **Keeps content maintenance focused.** If you've worked with large-scale content products, you know how hard it can be to wrangle editorial teams. A lack of planning or direction can lead to teams in different company silos generating duplicate content. Small but urgent updates end up published wherever—often as a brand new page, even when there's a more appropriate place available. A strict adherence to a single location for each focused topic helps point your content authors in the right direction.

- **Scales better.** Structure and navigation should be defined based on what the content is about and the natural links between each topic. Because you defined these relationships up front in your content model, you can populate each content type with unlimited instances of content without running into problems with your information architecture.

▪ **Makes content easy to find and share.** Your content is broken up and structured based on a well-researched model. Each resource is shaped around the kind of thing your audience is looking for. The way these resources are linked maps to how the real-world topics they cover really interconnect. Each resource is individually addressable, making it easy to locate in search or to share on social media.

APPLYING STRUCTURE TO RESOURCES

In Chapter 3, we looked at the unstructured content "blobs" found in traditional web publishing. Blogging platforms, such as WordPress, present the author with a WYSIWYG (what you see is what you get) editor. It has a title field for the title, and a body field for pretty much everything else. The author writes and structures their article on the page itself, adding subheadings, formatting, and links as they go. If we were to have created the IA Summit website in this way, the authoring interface might have looked like **FIGURE 7.1.**

FIGURE 7.1
Unstructured content in the body field is readable by humans but not by computers.

At first glance this doesn't look too bad. It's a page with all the relevant information. But the content lacks intelligent structure. You see the names and photos of two session hosts, but there's nothing going on behind the scenes to tell you that these mug shots belong to specific people holding the role of session host. You can see links on Kristina's and Karl's names, presumably to their profile pages. The author needed to add these links by hand. There's some important date and time information for the session, but again, it's been typed in manually by the author.

As created, all this information exists only on this one page. If you wanted to associate either of these people with another session, you'd have to make a new page for that session and add the names and photos all over again. If someone wanted to change a photo (or even a name), you'd have to visit every page they appear on and make those changes one by one. If the session time changed, you'd have to update it everywhere it appears.

The content is only *human*-readable. Humans are able to parse that page and infer the relationship between the session and its hosts. Humans can scan the text looking for salient details, such as date, time, and location. But to a computer, the entire body field is a big, unstructured blob of text. The computer can't understand the relationships and doesn't know that this session's "time" is a real-world time interval in a specific time zone. It doesn't know that the session will run in a specific venue, the same one that holds four other sessions that day. The computer has no idea that the hosts of this session are the same ones who ran some great workshops earlier in the week. It doesn't even know that this page is about a specific session.

With structured content, the computer does know. You've defined all those concepts and told the computer how they relate. Now it can help you with the heavy lifting. Change someone's profile photo, and the computer updates it everywhere that person appears. Tell the computer when each session starts and ends, and it will later help you build a dynamic schedule view. Move a session to another room, and push that change to everyone's computer and phone or to the venue's digital signage.

That's the power of structured content. Each concept is defined through its content type and constituent attributes. All these elements are connected intelligently based on the relationships you defined in your model. Rather than creating content in one big page-shaped blob, you'll instead create it in smaller chunks. Each chunk supports an attribute of a content type with specific content, such as the title, description, or host of a specific conference session. In your model, you've told the computer what a Session is and that it has a title. You've told it that Sessions have Hosts and that those hosts are people who have a name and photo and biography. So when you provide those names, photos, and biographies as separate chunks, the computer understands how they should fit together. Chunks can be reused over and over across different resources. And whenever they're updated at the source, those changes are reflected everywhere.

But back to the unstructured world for a moment. That enormous blob of content not only lacks computer-friendly intelligence but is also stuck in a specific page layout. What if you decided to offer a different subset of information on mobile? Or on a smartwatch? Or a kiosk? Using responsive design techniques will only get you so far. At worst, you could be forced to re-author pages for each device. That leads to issues of maintaining duplicate versions of content, which is an expensive and messy place to be.

With structured publishing, the content isn't trapped in the page. It lives outside any page representation at all. In fact, what might look like a single page is really made up of distinct chunks of content. Rather than laying out content directly, you design display *templates* for each content type. These gather together content for some or all attributes, using whatever layout and formatting options you choose. This frees you to design templates to suit the needs of each device. For example, with an Apple Watch app, you could limit a Session display to showing only the Session Title, Host, Venue, and Start Time. Admittedly, some representations, such as an Amazon Echo skill or a Facebook chatbot, stretch the definition of "template." But the principle remains the same: specific fragments of content returned in response to a user's inquiry.

USING CHUNKS TO DESIGN USEFUL CONTENT

In the sports car example from earlier, the Vehicle content type attributes include a name, a description, and photos and videos of the car in action. To publish a resource for the Porsche 911, you'd first design a general-purpose Vehicle template that reserves a space for each attribute. The computer would then fill out specific information about the 911 in each of these spaces (FIGURE 7.2).

You could choose to really flesh out the resource with coverage on the 911SC and Carrera variants (mapping to the Related Models attribute) and a biography of designer Butzi Porsche. More likely, though, you'd want to keep it focused on the 911 and make separate resources for related topics.

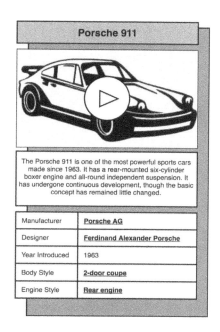

FIGURE 7.2
A Porsche 911 resource composed of attributes from the `Vehicle` content type.

As a designer, you can decide whether to display the content of your chunks within the same resource or to merely reference that chunk by linking off somewhere else. For example, you might choose to show a specification table where the `Rear Engine` attribute is listed, but link off to a separate resource describing rear-engine design.

With structured content, you can make those kinds of decisions while designing your templates. Any template can call upon any content chunk from any content type. The content flexes accordingly.

> **NOTE** Not to go all *Inception* on you, but sometimes a chunk could itself be a complete resource. For example, a YouTube video may be embedded in your web page, but it can also be linked to directly on YouTube. We tend to think of "resources" as things that can be identified or located via an address such as a Uniform Resource Locator—commonly known as a URL.

So let's return once more to the IA Summit site example and take another swing at the Session page. This time let's use attributes from the content model to compose a template. We'll illustrate this with content from a specific session, but really we want the template to be common to all sessions.

We've said that well-designed content is, above all, useful. It provides the answers people want to know. What questions does the audience have about a conference session? Your research has uncovered the top five questions:

- What's this about?

- What kind of session is it?

- Who's hosting it?

- When and where is it?

- What will I learn?

The content for each `Session` topic must answer these questions. A quick check of the content model confirms that you have all the stuff you need (**TABLES 7.2** through **7.6**).

TABLE 7.2 **WHAT'S THIS ABOUT?**

CONTENT TYPE	ATTRIBUTE	EXAMPLE CONTENT
Session	Session Title	A Tale of Twin Cities
Session	Session Description	Karl Fast and Kristina Halvorson in conversation. As the Information Architecture Summit visits content strategy's spiritual home of Minneapolis, let's look at how these disciplines compare, why they're important, and what they can teach each other.

TABLE 7.3 **WHAT KIND OF SESSION IS IT?**

CONTENT TYPE	ATTRIBUTE	EXAMPLE CONTENT
Session	Session Type	Fireside Chat
Session	Track	Masters of IA

TABLE 7.4 **WHO'S HOSTING IT?**

CONTENT TYPE	ATTRIBUTE	EXAMPLE CONTENT
Person	Name	Kristina Halvorson Karl Fast
Person	Photo	khalvorson-large.jpg kfast-large.jpg

TABLE 7.5 **WHEN AND WHERE IS IT?**

CONTENT TYPE	ATTRIBUTE	VALUE
Session	Session Date (Start)	04/26/15 10.00.00 AM
Session	Session Date (End)	04/26/15 10.45.00 AM
Venue	Name	Nicollet A

TABLE 7.6 **WHAT WILL I LEARN?**

CONTENT TYPE	ATTRIBUTE	EXAMPLE CONTENT
Session	Takeaway	How content strategy got big
		How editorial structure needs IA
		What IAs can learn from content strategists

Together, these chunks of content answer the user's questions. Every `Session` has the same set of attributes, filled with values specific to each instance. During interface design, you'll decide the relative layout and priority of the attributes or whether to include them at all (**FIGURE 7.3**).

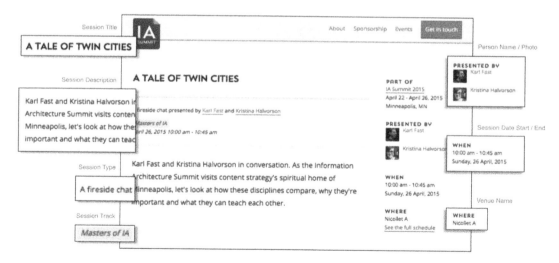

FIGURE 7.3 The session template composed using individual content resources.

Note that even though this is a template for the `Session` content type, it pulls in chunks from the `Person` and `Venue` content types too. Although you want to refer to Kristina and Karl only by their name and photo on this page, the computer knows they are actually full instances of the `Person` content type. So it can manage the automatic linking between this page and their respective Person pages. This is where all that work in modeling starts to pay off—with intelligent chunks of content, combined into dynamic templates.

PREPARE YOUR CONTENT

Now that we've looked at the basic principles of structured content design, you'll be eager to get your content chunks ready for assembly. Fortunately, you have a plan. You've put in the research legwork to determine the kinds of things your audience wants to see. You've used this to build a comprehensive model of the subject domain, and a more detailed structure of each type of content you want to support.

Whether you are starting from scratch or have piles of unstructured material ready to chunk up, your models now serve as a reference guide for designing useful and usable content.

AUDITING WHAT YOU HAVE

If you work in content strategy, you'll know all about content audits. Love 'em or hate 'em, they're a big part of the job. Auditing your inventory can be a laborious process. Firing up an enormous spreadsheet to examine every piece of content you have, before evaluating its worthiness for publication.

How old is it? How significant and useful? How original? The audit helps you identify high-performing content that deserves showcasing. It reveals gaps (or opportunities) in which to create new content to better serve the audience. And most often, it exposes a long tail of content that needs a good pruning. Without a plan, many businesses publish way too much information and leave it up forever. The audit exposes your ROT: redundant, outdated, and trivial content.

But how to decide what makes the cut? Hard evidence helps. Your web analytics will show the most and least popular content. Publishing dates identify items likely past their prime. (Treat content like food, with "use before" dates.)

But beyond that, determining value can be subjective. Let your domain model guide you. Examine every article, every video, every infographic. For each, ask if:

- **It maps to a content model attribute.** Let's say you're in the domain of `Baseball` and you have some content about Wrigley Field. Looks like a good instance of the `Venue` object described in your model. Of course you'll need to make sure it's good quality and up to date. But you're definitely in the right ballpark.

- **It doesn't map to a content model attribute or domain object.** Uh-oh, red flag. Assuming you have faith in your model, topics falling outside it may well be redundant. True story: A UK central government website had a section about environmental issues. It sprawled so much it started to include practical advice for beekeeping. Not so on-topic for government matters, perhaps.

  You could also decide that although the content in question doesn't map to one of your fleshed-out content types, it does relate to an object from the original domain model. In that case, revisit your models and consider defining a new attribute or even a whole new content type. It's perfectly valid to adapt the models in response to new information.

- **It kinda-sorta maps to several domain objects.** Is it a long video? Perhaps a very broad article? Chances are you have the makings of a good piece of content. Consider cutting, shaping, or editing it into one or more chunks, each of them squarely about one topic.

FINDING THE RIGHT CHUNK SIZE

Way back in Chapter 1, we told you about Tom, the BBC product manager responsible for their natural history website. Tom sifted the BBC television archives, looking back over 50 years of film and video to find just the right chunks content to fill out his product.

Each TV episode was a complete, edited documentary designed for broadcast. Episodes were usually around 45 minutes long and covered a broad theme, such as Africa, mammals, or dinosaurs. Episodes were constructed from several sequences, with each sequence made up of individual shots.

What's the best way to deal with this material? One approach is to put each 45-minute episode online and let people watch them in any order. After all, the BBC crafted these to be compelling pieces of television. But Tom didn't want a virtual VCR. He wanted to use this content to demonstrate how the natural world all joined up. He wanted individual resources for each animal and each type of habitat.

But the TV content wasn't focused enough to be suitable. A documentary about China would have fantastic footage of the giant panda but would later move on to look at otters and whales. So including the entire documentary in a resource for the giant panda doesn't fulfill the need to connect someone efficiently to relevant content.

At the other extreme, each documentary could be completely deconstructed. As it happens, the production notes for each show include an edit decision list, a complete record of the individual shots cut together. Tom could have wrenched every shot of a giant panda out of the show and put them one by one on his Panda page. He'd certainly meet the need for focused content, but at what cost? Those shots combine to form a self-contained narrative. Chopped up too much, it becomes moving wallpaper. That might be ideal for some products, but not the best choice for one designed to inform and educate—to say nothing of the expense and effort of making hundreds of video clips, each lasting only a few seconds.

The pragmatic choice is the middle ground. Each complete sequence is a visual paragraph. It provides useful information while keeping the narrative intact. The effort needed to clip sequences from the complete show seems proportionate to the reward. Some sequences that really, really aren't about "one" thing may end up on the cutting-room floor. But that's okay. Less content means greater focus.

Chunking should aim for what technical writers call "minimum reusable units," self-contained fragments that make sense on their own. Chunks are meant to be reusable. Each chunk may appear in many different page compositions. Your CEO's biography could find itself appended to every press release you publish. Your award-winning elephant footage appears today in your elephant resource. Tomorrow it also gets remixed into your special feature on the Serengeti.

The attributes of your content model tell you what each chunk should be about. When evaluating your unstructured content inventory, look for the things that

- Map to the attributes of your content types

- Are interesting (or at least make sense) when seen as a standalone unit

- Work across different devices (or have equivalent alternatives, such as a standalone audio soundtrack and text transcript for each video clip)

- Would provide valuable context to support other content (such as press office contact details on a press release)

Good chunks are valuable on their own, but even more valuable when assembled together. Chunking creates content assets (such as video clips) ideal for reusing within your own product and sharing on social media services. So craft each chunk to fulfill principles of good content design: focused, distinctive, and useful.

TROUBLESOME CONTENT

So far we've considered the most typical forms of content: text, photos, and videos. Apply structure to that stuff and you're most of the way home. But when you're dealing with your legacy web content, you'll probably come across a few problem children. Things that are technically "content" but don't exactly fit the bill. Here are a few examples we've had to deal with:

- **Photo galleries and carousels.** It's pretty common for websites to feature at least one large JavaScript-driven interactive gallery embedded on a page. The photo content becomes completely tangled up in its method of presentation. Separate them, you must. People don't care about photos because they're photos; they care about what those photos are about. This leads you back to your content model and its attributes. What thing does each photo describe? Does that thing have a content type? And does that content type have a `Photo` attribute? (Or even a complete `Photo` content type, with `Photo`, `Caption`, `Location`, and `Photographer` attributes?) You can worry about how to present these photos later. Right now it's more important to weave them into your content structure.

■ **Games and interactives.** Publishers like Disney and CNN often like to include rich interactive elements, such as Flash games or HTML5 dynamic infographics. It's best to treat these as chunks rather than try to disassemble them. You can still build them into your content structure, however, by adding a `Game` or `Interactive` attribute to a content type and treating them much like you would a video clip.

NOTE Even when chunking layout-based elements such as callouts, focus on meaning rather than presentation style. It's better to name an attribute `Summary` rather than, say, `Info Box`. Meaning travels across interfaces, but presentation styles can vary. Define your attributes based on what the content is *about*, not how it's presented.

■ **Pull quotes and callouts.** Ah yes, the other meaning of structured content—applying structure within a piece of content to give it visual hierarchy or additional meaning. Flip through this book and you'll see pull quotes, tips, and sidebars all supporting the main body text. If we were to ask a computer to apply consistent styles to each, we would, of course, need to identify what's what—hence, we add those attributes into our content types. You'll notice that for the conference session example in the last section, we identified `Takeaway` as an attribute separate from the main `Description`. That gives you the option to style `Takeaways` differently, or even leave them out of some representations completely.

■ **Tables.** Tabular information can be tough to deal with. Often you'll find that a table has been represented in HTML table markup but that it lacks any machine-readable structure that tells a computer what the values mean. Yet tables could benefit greatly from that structure, since you pretty much need a different design solution for every device just to display the data legibly. Painful as it may sound, the best approach is to define each row and column as an attribute. That work does pay off later, however. You've just told the computer what all the values in the table represent. Rendering the values as a table is now just one of your visualization options.

■ **Forms.** Whether it's to ask a question, make a reservation, or file a complaint, forms are traditionally how users talk to a business. A form is a way of gathering structured input that is stored in the tables of your content management database. Each form field should therefore map to an attribute. You probably already have these attributes scattered across your content types. For example, a restaurant may have modeled the concept of a `Booking`, which would include attributes such as `Name`, `Time`, and `Table Size`. Any input from a user-facing booking form would be stored using these attributes. It's the same thing with an inquiry, contact request, or complaint. By making this kind of customer feedback part of your model, you can better manage incoming information.

Auditing almost always throws up troublesome content, but armed with your content model it's nothing you can't handle. Remember the basic principle of separating the content itself from its means of presentation. Revisit and revise your model to add or amend attributes that support the valuable content you find. And consider that your model is based on research into what people want. This is a great opportunity to remove all content that is redundant, outdated, and trivial.

FILLING IN THE BLANKS

So you've done a complete audit and found some gaps in your content inventory—parts of your model that your audience has told you are super important but that you just don't have content for, no matter how much you chunk and reshape things.

Of course, your first approach is to create that content. You've already defined its topic, size, and shape—down to the last chunk. You've defined generalized content types and reusable display templates. Through modeling, you've even defined a scalable, interlinked structure. Each resource is consistently constructed from the same content attributes and linked together automatically. Content management just became easier.

CREATING NEW CONTENT

Day to day, every content author should be clear on what they'll create. The outline of your product is already there, waiting for authors to fill in the details. If that content team is already in place, they're going to experience a new, and hopefully improved, process of creation.

Once, Mike worked with a large publishing company. They'd been working the old way: disconnected pockets of the business making lots of independent, unlinked microsites. Lots of repetition and redundancy, and no clear publishing strategy. The site authors also were de facto designers, content strategists, and information architects. Every new microsite was designed and built from scratch, mostly ignoring the others surrounding it. The process was expensive, hard to scale, and not great for findability.

A move to structured content changed the workday of each author. The territory was well mapped. Even the structure and composition of individual pages were fixed in place and consistent. The expert content creators were free to focus on what they did best. Guided by the model, they created instances of content types, filling out every resource with the best text, audio, and video content available.

PLANNING FOR PRIORITY

Content strategists plan the regular production and publishing of useful, usable content. So it's typical to draw up an editorial calendar to align everyone tasked with making the content. If you're creating as a team, you'll need to prioritize what gets done first.

While the template-driven approach favors consistency, we all know that not all topics are created equal. In the domain of retro video-game consoles, it's way more important to have solid coverage of the Super NES and the Sega Genesis than it is the Apple Pippin or the Atari Lynx. Likewise, your Jane Austen app will probably have far more to say about *Sense and Sensibility* than about *Lady Susan*.

External events may also influence editorial priority. Anniversaries, movie releases, and notable deaths all tend to govern the specific content people come looking for. With an editorial calendar in place, you can anticipate some of these events (maybe not the deaths) and prepare content accordingly.

We should mention that not every resource needs an equal amount of content. Even though they may be based on exactly the same content type with exactly the same attributes, the Porsche 911 resource is probably going to end up much richer than the Muntz Jet. And that's fine, as long as the content type has sufficient attributes to be filled out later should more content become available. It's the same with Wikipedia articles—some just have much more to say than others.

UNCOVERING HIDDEN CONTENT

With the model as your treasure map, you know exactly what types of content you're looking for. The research that led to your model's creation may have uncovered a need for content never before published. But before you go ahead and create it from scratch, think about whether that content may lay hidden like buried treasure within your business.

It's not uncommon in a large business for valuable information or data to be collected and maintained somewhere far away from the eyes of the digital team. With a bit of digging into the business silos, who knows what you may turn up? For example, when we worked with a team making a music app for a radio station, some of the most valuable content came from the radio engineers. To manage royalty payments, they maintained a log of every song played on air. No one had considered the value of this data before. But the team connected it to profile content for each artist and created a wonderful music discovery service. People could look up their favorite artist and find out which radio shows were most likely to play them. Small, focused fragments of content could be lurking anywhere in the business. Think laterally.

LINKING TO OTHER SOURCES

If you need to reference certain facts but don't have them yourself, there's no shame in linking to someone who does. Even Wikipedia, with its self-contained articles, isn't averse to including footnotes to more authoritative sources. Linked content can still be considered part of your structured model. For any given content type, you could include an attribute for external links. That may be further fleshed out to include not only a URL but also a title and description. Sparse instances of the content type can then at least offer a help-ful and trustworthy link to another source. And should you later create content of your own, you're free to go back and improve those pages. In effect, you're using links to third-party content as a temporary placeholder for your own.

PUBLISHING ONLY WHAT YOU HAVE

Even with all your templates set up in advance, you don't have to publish empty pages or risk sending users down dead ends. Let's say you were build-ing the conference website but couldn't get the biography information for each speaker. You know who they are, but for some strange reason you don't have any details about them. In the model, the Person content type and its attributes are ready to take that content when you eventually have it. (And in fact you do have their names, so that's a start.) They're still an instance of the Person content type, just not a very complete one. So when you design your interface, you'll hold off on publishing Person pages until you have something more to put on them. Your Session pages can still include the name of each speaker as an intelligent chunk, but without any links to the (as yet unpublished) biography pages.

You've done a great job setting up all your structure in advance. But don't feel pressured to fill it with content all at once. You've set up the playbook that allows every content author to work consistently and efficiently. From here on in, your publishing schedule is up to you.

CONTENT FIRST, CONTENT ONLY

Adopting a structured content model doesn't affect only your content structure. It changes the content itself, forcing specialization and discipline. Each resource becomes dedicated to a specific thing. That focus helps you stick to principles of good content design. Remember, your content is most useful when it answers the questions people come looking for, when it's straightforward, and when it's easy to find and easy to share. If you're worried that this approach will result in a product that looks as visually sparse as Wikipedia, don't. Structured content can shine through rich and engaging website and app designs. Neither should you worry that you're about to flatten your product into a lifeless encyclopedia. While structured content doesn't impose rigid hierarchy, not every resource has to have equal emphasis. You'll be able to curate handpicked resources into special "collections" with an editor's flourish. So those home-page "featured stories" can still be driven by your content model. But more on all that in Chapter 9.

The structured approach also affects how content gets made. As you might have gathered from this chapter, we're not fans of WYSIWYG editors. We'd prefer that style decisions be part of a holistic design system, not made ad hoc by content authors. But there's no denying that if your content team has autonomy over how something gets styled or where it appears in a menu, then their world is about to change. We've seen authors feel disenfranchised by this. We've heard them talk about having their role reduced to "data entry." (They're entering content as fields into a content management system database, so technically this is true.) You may find yourself in need of diplomacy skills. Ask your authors to focus on their content expertise rather than their design enthusiasm. In return, you're providing a richly interlinked publishing platform—one where the authors' content has the potential to be found by, and thus help, more people. We'll bet that those people are coming for the quality content, not fancy interface design.

CHAPTER 8

IMPLEMENTING CONNECTED CONTENT

Bring the models to life! Just as with the rest of the process, building a content-first and model-based system requires a different mindset for your team. No handoff to the engineer. No big reveal from the designer. You're in this together, connected, just like your content.

FROM THEORY TO REALITY

Theory is done now. You've created your content strategy and determined what content needs to be made. It's time to get to work implementing a publishing system. Models are used to build the systems they were designed to represent. In this case, it's an information technology system that enforces the rules you've set for the collection, organization, and storage of content.

It's not enough to hand off the models with some notes about how you plan to create the content. As the person responsible, you need to continue to shepherd the content through implementation and visual design.

The evolution continues. From domain model to content model to defining specifications for the tool that will manage and publish your content—your content management system. What was a model of content types and attributes becomes a spreadsheet with details of not only each content type and its attributes, but also each *kind* of attribute: things like numbers, text, files, and images. Together with your engineers, you'll determine how best to set up the CMS to do whatever you want with the content chunks.

As you go from model to system specification, content types may transform to conform to the reality of your situation. Attributes may change as you think about representations and how the content will be used by visitors and entered by authors. That doesn't mean you did anything wrong before. You've only gotten more specific. You and your team continue to make decisions together. On with the show!

CONTENT MANAGEMENT AND THE CMS

Every day, millions of people create content. But not everyone who creates content manages it. And not everyone who manages it does it well. Content management is a discipline, as Deane Barker says in his book *Web Content Management* (O'Reilly). To manage content is to apply a set of theories, best practices, and accepted patterns. And it sure helps to have technology to help you do that.

As we explained in Chapter 3, structure underpins the implementation of your content-first process. You need a system to manage all those chunks. If you publish digital content, a CMS is the tool that lets you do that. Or maybe a product information management system is your tool. Or even a cobbled-together system of spreadsheets and data transfers. There is a wide range of choices to help manage the content that will be created based on your models.

TYPES OF CONTENT MANAGEMENT TOOLS

Not all content management tools are created equal. Whenever someone asks, "What CMS should I use?" or "What is the best CMS?" the answer is always, always, "It depends." Many tools can help you put your content on the web. What's best depends not only on your budget but also on how you want to manage your content and the skills your team has to build and maintain the system.

WEB PUBLISHING SYSTEMS

Want to get a website going without being a designer or understanding code? A web publishing system might be for you. The hallmark of this type of tool is that it allows you to create a bunch of web pages. With the magic of templates and widgets, you can pull together a great-looking website with content chunks and design elements dragged and dropped where you want them to end up. You might find a few elements of structured content that allow content reuse across the site, but mostly these tools create single-use web pages. Tools such as SquareSpace, Wix, and Weebly are perfectly fine solutions for some situations. But a web publishing system won't give you the structural flexibility for a structured-content, domain-driven approach.

WEB CONTENT MANAGEMENT SYSTEMS

To implement your content model effectively, you need a system that stores your content in a database, ready to reuse anywhere. Most of today's CMSs use a relational database to store structured content.

Here's the thing about our favorite CMSs: They pretty much start with nothing. A blank canvas. You get to make it all up! That seems daunting for someone who hasn't done a content model. But not you! You are ready for an approach to content management that allows you to manage content at the resource level, not at the page level. The goal is to create a set of resources with attributes that get pulled into different representations.

So there's no "best" or "right" one. But we do know that these qualities make for a solid CMS:

- Entity-based
- Customizable content types
- Separate design layer
- Third-party system integration capability
- Customizable user roles and permissions

Let's look a little more closely at the CMS qualities that support our approach.

Entity-based systems are those that allow you to create resources, as represented by your model. You set up each resource in the CMS and populate it with instance data. To create the display, just specify attributes from the content type to display in a template representation. Add a design layer to position and style each attribute. Design and content are completely separate here; you can even enter content before the design is finished.

In this type of system, the resources themselves don't change with the representation. That means you have more freedom in how to display or deliver your content. However many ways you want to represent something, you are choosing from the same set of elements.

This is the opposite of page-based systems that force you to create a hierarchical outline of your site (like in **FIGURE 8.1**, which shows how that is different from entity-based systems) and then create the pages one at a time. Resources can't be reused, because they're assigned to a specific spot in that outline. Admittedly, many page-based systems allow you to create structure within the page by chunking things into various segments. But they still put the representation first—you make a web page with a single objective. Instead of entities and content types, you lay out a web page. To create new content, you add a page to the directory and select a display template. Aggregating content requires an engineer to do programming rather than making some simple choices in the configuration settings.

Having a blank canvas for *free-form*, or *customizable, content types* is ideal. Because you've already mapped out how you want to set these up, you don't want to fuss with hacking what's already there. Hang on for how to set up your content types!

IA Summit 2015
▼ **Speakers**
    Jorge Arango
    Lynn Boyden
    Elizabeth Buchanan
▼ **Schedule**
    ► **Wednesday, April 22, 2015**
    ► **Thursday, April 23, 2015**
    ▼ **Friday, April 24, 2015**
        Opening Keynote
        The Crossover Role: PM + IA + UX
        Enterprise Taxonomy for FIFA
    ► **Saturday, April 25, 2105**
    ► **Sunday, April 26, 2015**
► **Minneapolis**
► **Team 2015**
► **Blog**

FIGURE 8.1 A tree structure for setting up the CMS (top) and an entity list (bottom).

🔍 Search   Content type ▼

Title ▼	Content Type ▼	Last Modified ▲
A History of the IA Summit	Blog Post	March 1, 2015
Kristina Halvorson	Person	February 21, 2015
Karl Fast	Person	February 12, 2015
A Tale of Twin Cities	Session	January 22, 2015
Hyatt Regency Minneapolis	Venue	January 10, 2015
Target Plaza Commons	Venue	January 10, 2015
Rosenfeld Media	Sponsor	December 1, 2014
2015 IA Summit	Event	November 30, 2014
Co-Chair	Role	November 30, 2104
Keynote Speaker	Role	November 30, 2014

To bring the content to the screen, a good CMS brings the interface design layouts and content together on-demand. Thus, it has a *separate design layer*, independent of the content. The design layer is the set of instructions for what the interface will look like. But there's no need to think about what it will look like yet, or even about what size screen or device will deliver the content, until you're ready to create a specific interface.

It is likely you have other systems you want to connect to, so *third-party system integration capability* is a must. Customer relationship management (CRM) tools, ecommerce software, customer service chat tools, and more form your digital ecosystem. Send data to and from the CMS so you don't have to duplicate it or manually update systems that share common data. For example, if all your product information is stored in your ecommerce software, create a data connection with the CMS to get the right information published to the website. When a new product is added or a price changes, the content author doesn't have to keep everything in sync. The system integration means that updates are sent to the CMS automagically.

The CMS should conform to your business and workflow rules, not the other way around.

A CMS should also allow you to *customize user roles and permissions* to access it. Maybe you want only the public relations manager to create the Press Release content type. Or you want the conference managers to be able to update the events calendar. Likely you have author, editor, and publisher roles, or other terms that define which users can publish content and which can only add or edit content. Each organization is different. The CMS should conform to your business and workflow rules, not the other way around.

THE HEADLESS CMS

The design layer could be so separate that you could skip it in your CMS altogether. A *headless CMS* is one without an embedded design layer. It's the pinnacle of separation of content and design! The CMS stores and delivers content to any interface application. The design—the front end, or *head*—gets applied at the point of display to the user through a separate system or codebase that pulls the content from the CMS into the representation.

Consider a headless CMS if you are truly ready to create a single resource per thing, want to manage that content in a single place, and want to publish across platforms. If you've come this far in the process, this is a viable option.

Some have said that the website is dying. But to paraphrase Mark Twain, reports of its death are greatly exaggerated. Still, there are many other ways of delivering content and only more to come. So if a CMS is strictly a *web* CMS, you'll miss a big opportunity. Ideally, the system will manage your content across all your platforms: websites and blogs, learning management systems, conference management systems, native apps, product information systems, and more. We like where this evolution is going.

> ## WordPress: A CMS or a Web Publishing System?
>
> WordPress, currently the most used tool for website publishing, might look like a full-blown CMS, but really it's just a glorified web publishing system. That's fine for a lot of teams, but using WordPress to implement model-based content requires custom development work. You start with a theme that includes a visual design template and a small set of content types with predefined attributes. Relationships between content resources and attributes are made through manual links, not inherent connections. Off the shelf, WordPress is great if you need only to publish a bunch of web pages. And it certainly offers the less technically savvy a solid publishing interface. But its focus on pages, rather than resources and attributes, limits the possibilities afforded by model-based structured publishing.

BUILD YOUR OWN CMS

What if none of the commercial systems fits your need? Some really advanced and digitally mature organizations have built their own CMS. National Public Radio (NPR) did this around 2012, when they established their "create once, publish everywhere" (COPE) process. No existing CMS fit NPR's operational or resource-based content model. Although there are a lot more options now, sometimes your needs are so specific that building your own system is the best bet.

You want to build your tool to fit the model, not model your content to fit the tool.

For this to be a viable option, be prepared to build the CMS that fits your needs exactly. A true proprietary CMS is not one you buy. If you buy a system that's already created, it's no longer just yours. If you do build your own CMS, be sure you aren't tied to a single vendor to maintain your content or the system that manages it. It's best to have the skills on your team to build and maintain the system. Creating the in-house engineering expertise ensures you will be able to continue to enhance the CMS as your business and content evolve.

Whatever system you use, think about how to manage your content before worrying about how the web pages will look. There is a time for that, but first you need to get the content management right. All CMSs come with their own quirks, to be sure. But you want to build your tool to fit the model, not model your content to fit the tool.

CONTENT TYPES—THE TECHNICAL SIDE

The content model contains content types. The CMS also contains content types. In the CMS they are the actual container for your content. They may be called something else in your CMS—entry types, data-entry forms, templates. Whatever you call them, they're the building blocks of your system. We'll keep on referring to these generic content containers as content types.

To start planning your technology implementation, go back to your model and decide which content types and attributes need to be exposed. What once were abstract domain objects, then further defined as content types, now become fields in a CMS. Relationships between the content types are expressed by connecting certain fields. The model provides the answers to how those relationships work, and it's a blueprint for all the kinds of content you might want to surface. A Session is hosted by a Person with the Role of Host. A Sponsor can sponsor an Event or a Session. A Person is the Author of a Blog Post. And so on.

We've finally come to the part when a spreadsheet makes sense. You're defining engineering specifications. Your engineering partners can build what you specify, but first they must understand the specifications you give them. Work with them. Be the advocate for content and the people who manage it.

AUTHOR SUPPORT

For the sake of simplicity, we'll use *authors* to mean the people who create and enter content into a CMS. These people may fill many roles, but what matters is their role in using the CMS. They are its users. Consider how they use this tool, whether it's every day or once a year.

The usability of the CMS is every bit as important as the technical attributes. You want flexibility in making the user interface, one the authors can actually use and that supports their content management efforts. Think of it as "training the CMS," as Eileen Webb says (https://alistapart.com/article/training-the-cms). There's a lot to remember, so rather than issuing a manual, build the guidelines and governance into the CMS itself.

Authors are not necessarily familiar with breaking up content into chunks for reuse. They may complain that they used to have more flexibility when there was just one big WYSIWYG editor for them to use. But structured content provides many benefits that are not obvious at first glance. Show them how putting these rules in place helps maintain consistency, makes it easier for them to enter content, and allows their content to be reused in various ways. All of this helps them to drive business success.

All the principles of user-centered design apply just as must to the back end of your CMS. Authors are your users too.

What's Wrong with WYSIWYG?

As we alluded to in the last chapter, we're not fans of the "what you see is what you get" (WYSIWYG) editor. Its main problem is right there in the name—an approach designed to make things look the same in the CMS as they do in the user interface. But combining interface design and content entry is missing the point.

WYSIWYG editors were created to help people mark up content without needing to learn code. But we now have sophisticated tools to apply code upon delivery to the interface rather than storing it with the content itself. We know that many authors—especially the ones who use the CMS rarely—like the comfort of the WYSIWYG editor because of its similarity to tools such as Microsoft Word. One of your many duties will be helping reluctant authors come to grips with field-based content entry. It's easier if you get them involved early in the content creation process, thinking about structure before they ever get to content entry. Sometimes it is appropriate to give them some formatting control, but limit the selections available: making text bold or italic, adding links, creating lists, applying heading styles, and selecting predefined CSS styles.

CONTENT TYPES IN THE SYSTEM

Use a spreadsheet to document the technical specifications for building content types. Our typical spreadsheet contains the following columns for specifications, but modify these to suit your needs.

- Content Type Name

- Description (what is this content type used for)

- Field Label (what each entry field is called)

- Data Type (technical term for the type of field this is)

- Notes

FIELDS

Each content type is a form in which each attribute becomes a form field. Each field has three components:

- **Label:** What the author sees as the name of the form field

- **Data Type:** Defines the kind of information that can be entered into a field

- **Value:** The actual information entered into a field

Think of this as form design. Forms are the interface layer between a user and a database. Borrow principles of information design and hierarchy, interaction design, and stakeholder management to make the content types easy to use and intuitive.

Back to the IA Summit. When the time came for us to plan the Session content type for our CMS, we started with our list of attributes:

- Session Title

- Person

- Description

- Takeaways

- Session Type

- Topic

- Time/Date

- Duration

- Venue

- Room

- Cost

- Sponsor

This was a good start. But as we planned the representation of each Session instance, we found we needed a few more things. See TABLE 8.1 for why we made changes when setting up the CMS. FIGURE 8.2 shows how it ended up coming out in the CMS.

TABLE 8.1 **DIFFERENCES IN CONTENT TYPES FROM CONTENT MODEL TO CMS**

MODEL ATTRIBUTE	CMS FIELD LABEL	REASON FOR DIFFERENCE
Session Title	Session Title	n/a
Person	Presented By	This label made more sense.
Description	Session Description	To be specific about what was being described.
Takeaways	Session Takeaways	To be specific about what takeaways were to be listed.
Session Type	Session Type	n/a
Topic	Session Track	We didn't have well-defined topics, just a loose collection of sessions that had similar themes or formats.
Time/Date	Session Date (start)	To provide a start and end time specifically, these needed to be divided up (date field types include time).
	Session Date (end)	
Duration	Workshop Length	Duration was automatically calculated with start and end date and time, but we wanted to state whether a workshop was full- or half-day.
Venue	Location	We combined these into a single field because all but a few sessions are in the same venue.
Room	Location	
Cost	Cost	n/a
	Sold Out	We needed a way to let people know when a workshop was full.
Sponsor	Session Sponsor	To be specific that this was for the session.
	Main Event	To link it to a particular instance of a conference.
	Comment	The co-chairs also wanted to say why a session was valuable or give some sort of commentary.

FIGURE 8.2 The
`Session` content
type in the
Drupal CMS.

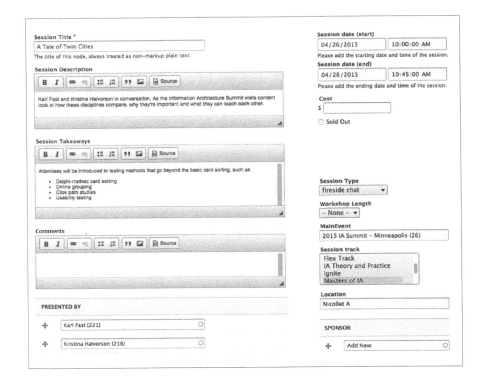

TECHNICAL ATTRIBUTES (DATA TYPES)

Your content management system is a database. That means you also have
to define *data types* (**TABLE 8.2**), or what kind of field each of these attributes
needs to be, and assign one to each attribute. The good news is that there
aren't many of them. There might be some variance from system to system, but
keep this list handy to endear you to your engineering team.

Use these field types when defining attributes for content types in your CMS or
information system's database.

TABLE 8.2 **DATA TYPES FOR CMS FIELD SPECIFICATIONS**

DATA TYPE	DESCRIPTION
Boolean	One of two values *Examples: Yes/No, True/False*
Date	An entry as an ISO date or Unix timestamp; includes date and time
Email	Email address; turns addresses into *mailto* links
Entity reference	To select instances of another content type
File	Reference to a file in the file system of the CMS *Examples: PDF, Excel worksheet, Word document*
Image	Reference to an image file
Link	For storing and validating URLs
List (text)	List of text options (can be formatted as either a drop-down list or checkboxes)
List (float)	Drop-down list of floating decimals
List (integer)	Drop-down list of integers
Number (Integer)	A whole number, such as a year (*example: 2012*) or value (*examples: 1, 2, 5, 305*); does not allow decimals
Number (Float)	A number that can use decimals *Examples: 0.012, 138.7, 200.87*
Number (Decimal)	A number that allows *exact* decimal values; often used for price *Example: $199.99*
Term reference	Reference to an existing taxonomy term
Text (plain)	Short text (limited to 255 characters) *Examples: Name, Title, Company*
Text (plain, long)	Long, multiline alphanumeric text (no HTML tags allowed)
Text (formatted)	Text field with rich text editor (basic HTML tags allowed)
Text (formatted, long with summary)	Same as formatted text, but with an additional summary text field

From the IA Summit content model, the technical specifications for the `Session` content type looked like **TABLE 8.3**.

Repeat this process for each content type. Just as when you went from domain model to content model and split up and merged objects, you may do the same at this point with content types and attributes.

There's no rule about the minimum or maximum number of fields to use or how many content types you should have in your system. Be like Goldilocks: Have just enough fields so that it is intuitive for an author to use when entering content and for the content to translate to the display properly.

TABLE 8.3 **DATA TYPES FOR CMS FIELD SPECIFICATIONS**

NAME	DESCRIPTION	FIELD LABEL	FIELDS/TYPES
Session	Holds information related to individual sessions (workshops, socials, keynotes, etc.)	Session Name	Text (plain)
		Description	Text (formatted)
		Presented By	Entity reference (**Person**)
		Session Type	Term reference (**Session Type**)
		Workshop Length	Term reference (**Workshop Length**)
		Cost	Number (decimal)
		Sold Out	Boolean (Yes/No)
		Session Date (start)	Date
		Session Date (end)	Date
		Location	Text (plain)
		Main Event	Entity reference (**Event**)
		Session Track	Term reference (**Session Track**)
		Takeaways	Text (formatted)
		Comment	Text (formatted)
		Session Sponsor	Entity reference (**Sponsor**)

RELATIONSHIPS

You may have noticed the entity reference data type in Table 8.3 and that it was used many times in the `Session` content type definition. And you might be scratching your head over this one. Let's back up and explain. An *entity* is a thing or concept that is unique, distinguishable, and self-contained. A *reference* is something that points to another thing. An entity reference is the center of the content relationships. When you use an entity reference (or whatever your system calls this type of field), you are saying to the database, "I want to connect this instance of the thing I'm creating to that instance of another type of thing." In this case, when creating the `Session` instance for A Tale of Twin Cities we selected Karl Fast and Kristina Halvorson from the `Person` content type in the `Presented By` field. Now the computer knows that these things are related and can make all kinds of inferences from them.

That's nice for the computer, but it's also nice for you. It means you can create less content. Instead of entering the `Host`'s information with the `Session`, you've already entered it as a `Person` and all you need to do is select the right name from a list. In the display of a `Session`, you can pull in any attributes about the `Host` that you want. Likewise, you also can pull in attributes from the `Session` to the `Person`'s biography page, which is exactly what we did on the IA Summit website (**FIGURES 8.3** and **8.4**).

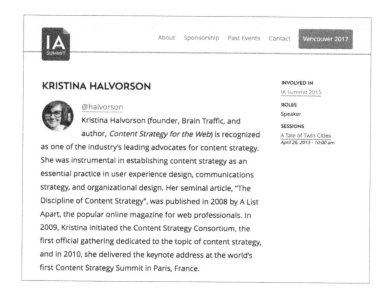

FIGURE 8.3
Person display shows **Session** info.

FIGURE 8.4
`Session` display shows `Host` info.

Guess what else? Change the name of the session, and it gets changed in every relationship. If a person gives you a new photo, it gets uploaded once and displayed wherever that person's photo appears in the interface.

In the longer term, this relationship building has even more benefits. For the IA Summit, it might be tempting to think only of a single year's event. But as we've pointed out, the same people hold different roles from year to year. This year's co-chair could be last year's workshop speaker and next year's keynote speaker. With the `Person` content type, the information about the person stays the same no matter what the year and the role. A new relationship with the new instance of an `Event` and a `Role` can be created without re-entering personal information. Just go to the `Person` entry and choose the new `Role` once they sign the keynote speaker contract.

Having these relationships means you must think about which way they flow. In the `Live Music` domain, does a `Performer` belong to a `Lineup` or does a `Lineup` have `Performers`? Since the `Performer` always has the same values no matter which `Lineup` they belong to, it would make sense to have `Performer` as an entity reference in the `Lineup` content type (**TABLE 8.4**).

`Performer` has no entity references in its attributes, at least not in the `Live Music` domain. That content type only describes the `Performer`. A `Performer` can have many relationships through the `Lineup` reference for reuse in various representations (**TABLE 8.5**).

TABLE 8.4 **CMS SPECIFICATIONS FOR LINEUP**

NAME	DESCRIPTION	FIELD LABEL	FIELDS/TYPES
Lineup	Brings together individual performers for a specific combination	Lineup ID	Number (Integer)
Group	The collective group or band represented by this lineup	Group	Entity reference (`Group`)
		Performers	Entity reference (`Performer`)—allow multiple

TABLE 8.5 **CMS SPECIFICATIONS FOR PERFORMER**

NAME	DESCRIPTION	FIELD LABEL	FIELDS/TYPES
Performer	Individual who puts on shows	Full Name	Text (plain)
		First Name	Text (plain)
		Last Name	Text (plain)
		Birthdate	Date
		Birthplace	Text (plain)
		Birth Name	Text (plain)
		Biography	Text (formatted)
		Genre	Term reference (Genre)
		Photo	Image
		Website	Link

TAXONOMY—A QUICK NOTE

We'd be doing structured content a disservice if we left out taxonomy. Officially, a *taxonomy* is a classification of information into ordered categories. When it comes to digital content, taxonomies allow you to organize, categorize, and relate content. Apply them to various content types and you can hook them up by matching terms. The `Person` content type in which the `Role` is `Keynote Speaker`. `Performance` with the `Genre` of `Indie Rock`. `Vehicle` with the `Style` of `Coupe`. Some of the content types from the model are really taxonomies that allow you to classify other content types.

A content type can be classified in many ways. A `Recipe` has ingredients, a type of food, a preparation style, a season, and preparation ease. And you could assign any or all of those a value for a chocolate chip pumpkin muffin recipe and find it in many places, depending on how you wanted to discover it: pumpkin, breads, baking, autumn, and easy. This is the beauty of digital classification: You don't have to decide on just one categorization, like you do with paper (Carrie keeps it in the Breads category of her recipe binder).

A taxonomy shows intent. You define the terms in a taxonomy based on how you want to position your content in your domain, or even in the wider world. For the giant panda, the location could be China, Asia, or Yangtze. Just be sure you pick the level to classify all the instances of `Animal` the same way: country, continent, or region. Do you classify it as a bear (*Ursinade*), or do you put it in the same genus as the raccoon (*Procyon*)? Classification opens up debate, and with each decision you take a side. Be deliberate.

Whether people want to search or browse, a solid taxonomy improves findability and discoverability by allowing them to choose their own path. Most internal search engines allow for faceted narrowing by any number of things, from content type (book, journal article, blog post) to publication year to topic and beyond. Visitors who don't know exactly what they want can narrow the selection by choosing which facets to apply to their search.

Since you've created your navigation structure based on resources and your content model, it's easy enough for someone to start at the top of one of the categories and make choices all the way down when they want to explore by browsing. What to do with all that July corn on the cob from the farmers market? Start at seasonal foods, click on summer, easy, and main dish. Bam! Basic corn chowder for dinner! Or just as easily, choose side dishes instead. Bam! Creamed corn. Hungry yet?

The benefits of taxonomy and using it to bring your model to life go on. But that is for you to discover when you create your interface. When you're building your CMS, decide how to classify the content and make sure the terms will be easily understood by authors when selecting appropriate terms during content entry.

Taxonomies may manifest themselves in many ways, including metadata. *Metadata* is machine-readable information that describes a thing. It is descriptive and structural syntax for your fields. Some metadata is standardized for interoperability. Schema.org and Dublin Core are two of the most common metadata vocabulary sets. The good news about this is that your CMS may have this built into its core code and will do the work for you if you choose the right data types. For example, choosing the `Date` data type automatically applies the worldwide ISO standard that allows any computer to understand the values in this field as a date and time.

Taxonomies are woven into the fabric of your content. They can be as simple as select lists or checkboxes. Or they can be complex sets of terms that guide an entire domain. They can be hierarchical or flat. Whatever they are for your content, take full advantage of them.

CONTENT CREATION

The skeleton of your content is ready to be filled in. At last, you can start creating the content. And it's important to start doing that as soon as possible. You'll want to use sample content and start to enter it early to make sure it's all doable—that the authors understand this new way of creating content and that the system is indeed set up to accept and display it in a way that makes sense for the user.

STRUCTURED AUTHORING

You probably get that writing big blobs is not the way to fill out your content model. What was once a blob becomes chunks, which means that the people who write the content need to approach their writing differently. First, get the authors thinking about how these pieces fit into the bigger picture. If they are used to writing web pages, you'll need to coach them about techniques that we covered in Chapter 7 about designing content, not just writing it.

To help authors wrap their head around this structure, provide a guide for them. We call these *content spec sheets*. They specify the nature and structure of the content to be created. You can use a Microsoft Word document with a table that mirrors your structure (**FIGURE 8.5**). Include governance notes in them.

Content Spec Sheet template

Resource Name

Objective: brief statement of objective

Source of content: where content is coming from

Session Name (H1)	Resource Name
Description	Actual copy to be inserted into CMS
Takeaways	Things attendees will get out of the session (bullets)
Presented By	Who is hosting/speaking?
Session Type	Workshop, Keynote, Concurrent Session, Social Event, Meal
Workshop Length (Chose one)	Full-Day Half-Day
Cost	$XXX
Session Date & Start Time	MM/DD/YYYY HH:MM AM/PM
Session Date & End Time	MM/DD/YYYY HH:MM AM/PM
Session Location	Room, Venue (if not hotel)
Session Track	Masters of IA, Organizational Design, Career Path, Communicating Ideas, Case Study, Consulting, Mentoring, Networking
Comment	Anything to add about the session
Session Sponsor	If there is one
Page Title (meta)	Page Title – 70 characters or less

Content creation implications:

list any assumptions or notes about things that are affected by this resource

If you have a big team and lots of content, use a content production tool like GatherContent to organize, produce, and manage the production process. A pre-CMS tool like this can also export directly to some of the more popular CMSs.

CONTENT ENTRY

Start entering content into your system as soon as possible. You'll want to do this to make sure everything is working as planned. Start with a set of sample content. Decide how many instances of each content type you need to test to know that the content fits into the CMS just right. Having the right combination of sample content will also help when it comes time to create and test the different interface representations.

This might sound simple enough, but sometimes it takes a little extra brainpower. When we were deciding how many entries we needed to test `Person`, we had to consider all the roles and where the `Person` content type needed to be displayed. That meant we needed at least two of a bunch of different combinations:

- Role = `Co-chair`
- Role = `Team Lead`
- Role = `Peer Reviewer`
- Role = `Host`, Session Type = `Keynote`
- Role = `Host`, Session Type = `Session` or `Workshop`

Having all these instances would let us know whether the resource displays were correct. It would also let us see if the Speaker and Team indexes that list those groups separately were ordered and displayed as intended.

If it all comes out the right way, carry on! If not, make some changes and try again until it all works for the authors and the system and the delivery to the interface. Now development and design can continue in parallel with content creation and entry.

Use your spreadsheet to track progress on the content types. We include columns to track progress of the build:

- Set Up
- Sample Content Entered
- Content Quality Assurance (QA)

We also create columns for tracking content creation for each instance to make sure we don't miss anything:

- Author
- Content Written
- Content Entered
- Reviewed in Final Interface

There's a lot to track. Having one place where everyone can go to see progress and next steps keeps things moving.

ASSEMBLE THE IMPLEMENTATION TEAM

Planning and implementing connected content isn't for a team of one. We're not saying you can't use the information in this book to create better products and put your company on the right path. But it really does take a village; expertise in project management, design, development, and writing all combine to pull this together.

Earlier you worked with subject domain experts. You pulled from their heads everything you could about the domain and expressed it in your models. Designing a CMS around that model shifts you into design-team mode. We use the term "design team" very loosely. There's no universal term for the group of people who come together to implement a digital product. We like to use "design" in its purest sense: the plan and process of bringing something into the world. Therefore, the design team are the group of people who plan and create a product.

While this team lays the foundations for the CMS, the experts and stakeholders get a break. But don't go off into a cave, only to emerge once you're finished. There should be no "big reveal" of the CMS, declaring it ready for content. No presentation to your senior leadership team of mockups of a home page. No command to create some content for the website. Instead, use the process outlined in this book to include everyone continually who has a stake in the end product (you knew they were called "stakeholders" for a reason, right?):

- Product and project managers

- Engineers

- Front-end developers

- Designers

- Marketing/communications teams

- Senior leadership

- Stakeholders (content owners and authors)

- Content strategists

What is the role of each member of the design team? It might seem self-evident what the designers and engineers do, but humor us. Let's also be clear that these are roles, and an individual person may play several roles.

Product manager or **project manager:** Usually the product manager or project manager is in charge of the process. Whichever one you have on your team, they control the levers of the implementation players—who does which task, how much time they have—as well as managing the communication with the people outside that team. With lots of coordination, check-ins, and collaboration, they will bring the people and process together for a successful delivery.

Engineer: The engineer is the one who sets up the technology that delivers your content and interface to a user on their device. This includes the CMS or other information system that stores your content as well as the server that connects it all to the internet. The engineers should be involved in creating the content model to head off complications that could occur later in the process.

Front-end developer: The front-end developer writes the code that makes up the user interface. They're usually the HTML, CSS, and JavaScript experts. They might even be the person responsible for the "skin," or theme, of the CMS. You've given your content meaning by assigning attributes. Front-end developers translate the content model to HTML and JavaScript and then assign CSS to describe how each element should appear.

Designer: The designer shapes the experience, in part by orchestrating the details of the interface. From the overall graphic aesthetic to the cause and effect of interaction, they help to craft a positive experience for the user and generally make sure people notice all the right things. It's not just about making the product look good; it's about breathing life into the structure underneath.

Marketing or communications: The marketing or communications team defines the target audience, determines the message, manages the publishing schedule, and determines a dissemination or publishing strategy. They may even create content. If this is a separate group where you work, don't wait until the end of a project to bring these professionals in. Since they're responsible for helping your audience discover your content, they need to understand the content model and even contribute to its development.

Senior leadership: These are the decision-makers. The bosses' bosses. If you work at a bigger organization, you might not have much contact with these people. But you need to find a way to get their attention and buy-in. They are a relatively small group of people (with varying titles), but they can kill a project. Don't wait until you're almost done to show them your work. Early on, explain how your work helps the organization become more efficient and effective. Most likely, they care not about *how* so much as about *so what*. However, if you have to change the patterns of work or relationships between teams, they need to be onboard very early to support the changes. You don't want to go to all this effort only to be told "never mind."

Engage them at critical decision points:

- When you start the process—they may even be some of your domain experts

- When you have an early prototype or minimally functional product

Since everything is based on content and how that is best supported for use by your audience, they really only need a tour of what you've created. And a reminder of the *so what*. What is going to be different when this launches? How will this help the organization? And, for the chief operating officer, how it is built with a process that makes your internal team or your relationship with vendors better?

Stakeholders: These folks own the content. You've been working with them all along. First they were among your expert interviewees. Then they helped validate the domain model and ensure that the content model represents the right types of content. Now they approve the content that gets published. Keep them engaged. Content could be how their own success is judged. Does it help them meet their goals? Can they better serve their customers, clients, members, donors, advocates, or funders?

Content strategists: Maybe this is you, if you are the person who shepherds the content from conception to infinity. Content strategists serve many functions, depending on the organization and the team, but on the design team they champion content that is user-focused, aligned with business goals, and properly structured for reuse.

There are myriad others who could be involved: information architects, copywriters, account managers, business analysts, UX researchers, data analysts. The bottom line is this: Talk to others. Invite them into the process when it makes sense or when you need their expertise to make it all come out right. Involve them and you'll make allies, if not advocates.

EVERYTHING IS CONNECTED

Despite the linear format of this book, this process keeps a lot of plates spinning at once. Content creation, design, and engineering happen in parallel. Iteration comes at every step. As you create content, you sometimes realize that certain interface design choices would improve its usability. When the CMS is built, engineers find quirks in the system that require a rethink of some of the content types or fields. When coding the responsive templates, the front-end developer may discover that the images aren't suitable for high-definition display. And the more content you add, the more likely you are to find exceptions to all your rules. It's no big deal if you start small, have clear directions, and test early.

You've probably noticed that we're saving interface design for last. It certainly isn't least. You just needed to get all the content organized and structured for the design to be applied. It's like the frosting on a multilayered cake. The cake is delicious and stands up on its own, but something is missing that pulls it all together.

CHAPTER 9

BRINGING YOUR CONTENT TO LIFE

You've come far on your journey to design connected content. You've mapped out how your subject domain works and translated concepts into fine-grained content types and attributes. A plan that began as scribbles and sticky notes is now realized through a fully configured CMS. And best of all, you have compelling and focused chunks of content that perfectly describe each of your intended content resources.

Or maybe not. More likely, you're in hacked-together prototype mode. You have a domain model that could be better if only you had more research time. Your content types seem about right, but you're not totally sure you captured all you need. And your content gathering is far from complete, but you've put in some representative bits and pieces to test the CMS.

Abstract planning is difficult, especially when your stakeholders just want to see content working within a web page or app. Let's give them what they want. You've designed the content resources. Now you'll design the interface representations to display them to the world. All that carefully structured content roiling under the surface now bursts onto the screen. Enough with the content planning and structuring—it's showtime.

DESIGNING WITH CONTENT

A well-designed interface helps people make better sense of content. It encourages them to explore. Since form follows function, the interface should not detract or distract from the information it contains. After all, the content is why people come.

In this chapter, we'll go through our process for interface design. It's a process that takes the content structure you've now completed and layers on top each representation of the content. While this isn't a crash course in aesthetic layout and styling, we'll cover some of the basics of how content gets to the screen—and beyond. You might want to share these ideas with your resident UX or interface designer and figure out how you can work together to bring the content to life.

We'll also look at some of the technical implementation plumbing, including how to plan the URL addresses for your web resource. The details of how the content gets piped out to the interface are specific to your development environment and CMS, so discuss this section with your engineers too.

Whatever your CMS, you'll use a series of templates to show off your content to the world. The reusable template (think of it like a stencil) sets up a structure common to every resource of the same type so that you don't have to compose each of your content resources individually. The template governs the layout and styling of each content element. When the CMS publishes a resource (such as a web page about the Porsche 911), it takes your pieces of content and fits them into the spaces in the template.

Template-based design isn't without its challenges. You're asking a designer to create a layout that best serves the content, but with only a general sense of what that content will be. The design has to continue to work well even for content yet to be created. To preserve their sanity, the designer will often produce mockups based on one or two specific examples. They want the mockup to look good, so they choose examples that have the most complete information, the most luscious photography, and the most compelling topics. This is super, if that's truly representative of your content. More likely, your resources are a mixed bag. Some will have a ton of rich information and exciting media. Others (probably many others) will be relatively scant on detail. Your template design has to love these forsaken children too.

When you design your interface templates *after* designing your content, you have a huge advantage. Content itself becomes design material. The interface can be designed around the actual content it's there to contain. When you position and style visual elements powered by "live content," you see instantly whether that photo element deserves to be quite so large when the story is "Cat Stuck in Tree Horror!"

The Structured Content Stack

Product engineers like to talk about "stacks": the layers of detail that together make up the product experience. The popular model-view-controller stack for software architecture separates applications into three layers. The model holds all the data about rules and relationships. The view is a representation of the model's data, shown to the user. The controller allows the user to provide input.

In a similar sense, the structured content approach can be thought of as layers (**FIGURE 9.1**): domain and content models providing underlying structure, content illustrating that structure with examples, and everything shown through the interactive interface representations across devices. Your design is coming together from the bottom up. The interfaces you create are views onto the structured content beneath. Update the interface, or build a new one, and the content structure remains intact.

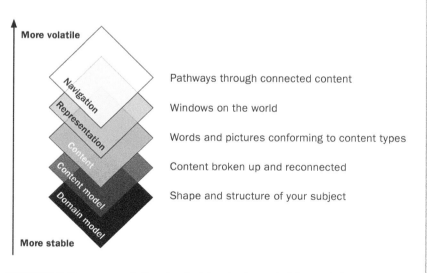

More volatile

Navigation — Pathways through connected content

Representation — Windows on the world

Content — Words and pictures conforming to content types

Content model — Content broken up and reconnected

Domain model — Shape and structure of your subject

More stable

FIGURE 9.1 The representation view is driven by the underlying model.

DEVISING DEVICE STRATEGY

You must be fed up with planning by now, so our apologies—designing interfaces takes a little preparation of its own. As a team, you'll need to figure out which devices you're designing for and then identify the templates you'll need for each.

Around your home, you probably have half a dozen different means of consuming digital content. Where once the desktop web browser was king, the balance has shifted in favor of mobile devices. Mobile itself is a fractured channel. The smartphone affords both browser-based content and native applications, and even the notion of *mobile* itself is expanding to watches, tablets, in-car interfaces, and whatever comes next.

Devices such as the Amazon Echo and Google Home have made popular a new category of screenless interface: the voice UI. These challenge our ideas of what interface design can be and certainly support the case for separating content from presentation. Likewise, interactive agents such as Siri and the chatbots exploding on Facebook Messenger offer a completely different interaction behavior for requesting and navigating content.

Interfaces, whether for screen or voice, are windows on the world. They each peer into the same structured network of content you've created, and each offers a different lens for interpreting and consuming that content. Your audience research may offer clues as to where to start. How do people most often access your current information? Where do you want to reach them? Avoid the temptation to want to be on the latest hot device just because it excites you. We've worked in digital long enough to remember clients insisting, "We need a website!" (with no underlying strategy) and then some years later, "We need an app!" (with no underlying strategy). As we write this, the rallying cry is, "We need a chatbot!" (And you guessed it...)

And sure, with structured content under the hood, you're in great shape to publish to all kinds of places. But be realistic. Every interface you create brings a whole set of design considerations and maintenance overhead. It's another child to raise. Start simple, supporting just one or two devices. You'll be able to test reaction and work out any kinks before eventually planning a wider rollout strategy. Even services like Netflix, which these days seems to be on everything from your cable box to your toaster, started out with just a desktop website.

GOING NATIVE

Designing with content may lead to a shift in how your designer usually works. It's common practice for designers to create mockup templates in tools such as Sketch or Adobe Illustrator. These blueprints are passed to an engineer who attempts to re-create them in code.

Without wanting to get bogged down in a debate on whether "designers should code" (go visit Twitter for that argument, unless you value your time and serenity), we do think there are huge advantages to laying out and styling your templates using the native fabric of the medium. If you're building web pages, that means designing with HTML and CSS. Mockups certainly have their place, but they're decidedly disconnected from your live content. That's why the designer has to cherry-pick some examples and copy-paste them into their file. That might be fine to get started exploring creative solutions, but the design isn't truly complete until content meets code. That's when you see whether the template really works for every content example you can throw at it.

Working this way doesn't necessarily mean sending your designer off to coding summer school. All along, you've tried to bring the disciplines of your team closer together. Template design can often look like a designer and an engineer sitting together, solving layout challenges as a creative team. It's a lot more effective than passing documentation down a production line. Try different ways of working to discover the best dynamic for your team.

PLANNING YOUR TEMPLATES

Digital content presentation relies on two things: resources and indexes. *Resources* hold your content, and *indexes* gather it together into lists. The two are closely related. A resource is a specific example of a type of content (like the Porsche 911), whereas the index will gather links to resources of a common type (for example, Vehicle). For each device, designing an interface starts with figuring out which resource and index templates you need.

Consult your content model. You've already defined each content type you could make available. For example, in the IA Summit content model, we had content types for

▪ Event

▪ Venue

- Sponsor

- Role

- Person

- Session

- Blog Post

From the list of content types, decide which should be graced with their very own template. Not every type needs a fully fledged resource to be published. The website didn't need pages describing each `Role`, and we didn't have enough content to justify creating a page for each `Sponsor`. The `Venue` content type held useful information, but that content might be better presented as a sidebar to other templates, rather than having a template of its own.

In the end, the only resource templates we created were for

- Person

- Session

- Blog Post

These were the most commonly referenced content types. Together they hold the vast majority of the content. You may similarly discover that you can cover your content inventory with just a handful of different templates. For consistency, and for pragmatism, fewer is better.

Index templates contextualize these resources. At the most basic, you could offer a general index for each content type (for example, a list of all the sessions or blog posts). But things get more exciting when you publish indexes based on the specifics of the content itself. Indexes come in many guises:

- The lineup of speakers at a conference

- All the shoes available in an online store

- Today's top news stories

- An interactive map of Civil War battlefields

- The 100 greatest movies of all time

Anytime you're collating and linking to multiple resources, that's an index. The very act of gathering particular resources together conveys some information about how these things are related. Our own speaker lineup was an index for the `Person` content type, but with the display limited to people who held the role of `Host` or `Keynote`.

Even the order in which the resources are prioritized can make the index a destination in its own right. For the IA Summit website, we ordered the `Session` index chronologically, based on the `Session Date (Start)` attribute of the content type. With the right template design, the index becomes an automatically updated schedule—perfect for pushing out those last-minute changes to attendees.

A SENSE OF PLACE

In *Every Page Is Page One*, former journalist Mark Baker argues that with web content, unlike with print media, any page could be the start of your reader's experience. With some exceptions (news and social media sites, for example), gone are the days of people arriving to the home page and navigating their way to the content they want. Google is pretty much the only home page that matters. After that, probably Facebook. Content resources are indexed by robots and shared by friends. People identify the content they're looking for and jump directly to that content resource.

Each resource should map neatly to the things that people search for. Fortunately, your research, modeling, and audience-friendly terminology have helped take care of that. But now here they are, parachuting into your page. A stranger in a strange land. What questions does your visitor need answered?

Is this the content I was looking for?

This is a content resource after all, so providing relevant information is job one. Thanks to some effective content design, you have crisp and compelling content that stays exactly on topic. Do all you can to showcase this content—it's why your visitor is here. It should be the most prominent visible thing, not obscured by navigation, related content upsells, or advertising. And within that content, aim to put the most pertinent information first. Consider the journalist's trick of the *inverted pyramid*—a summary of the most important details up front that precedes a more in-depth explanation.

How does this content relate to the domain?

Your visitor arrived at your content because of their wider interest in a particular topic. To get their bearings, they'll want to understand where this resource sits in a wider context. How the part relates to the whole. You have all that context from your model. You just need to express it. Label each resource with the kind of thing it is. Tell them that the Porsche 911 is a sports car or that the duck-billed platypus is a monotreme. Explain in your Jupiter resource that it was visited by the space probes *Voyager 1* and *Galileo*. Such facts should not be limited to the body of your content but expressed as related concepts—the relationships first defined in the domain model are now made explicit in the interface. Make those related concepts links to other resources and you have a contextual navigation model allowing people to explore the subject through its natural connections.

Where am I anyway?

Every page is page one, right? This means that, for web content at least, every content resource has to serve double duty as a pseudo home page. Not only do you need to make it clear that your visitor has arrived at the right content, but you also need to signpost the place they've arrived to. This is more than just branding. Of course you'll have your logo up top, but you also want to convey your product's proposition. What can people *do* here, and how is that made obvious by the information on display? What impression does the design give about the quality and reliability of that information? Your design choices contribute to the level of trust and satisfaction visitors will have with your content and, by extension, your product.

DESIGNING TEMPLATES

Okay, let's get hands-on now with designing resources and indexes. For each, you'll first create a basic, unstyled template to hold your content. You'll then position the elements of your content to bring a sense of order and priority and then style those elements with all kinds of visual loveliness.

From here on, we'll focus on HTML representations. That's the most popular way of presenting web-based content within desktop and mobile browsers, specialist devices such as kiosks, and even some native smartphone applications. But don't worry—even when you're using Swift or Java to create apps for iOS or Android, the same principles hold: Plan the representations you want, build out basic versions of each, and then position and style the content within them.

We'll assume your CMS is set up and has at least some sample content ready to be displayed. Let's assume too that you've figured out which templates you need (though don't worry—it's normal to add more or change these around throughout the design and build process).

THE SUPER-BASIC RESOURCE TEMPLATE

Let's construct a resource template for the Person content type. This reusable template will be pressed into service for every single person we want to publish a resource about. Start by making a very basic HTML document for the CMS to populate with content.

Once again, we're going to need to gloss over specifics. How HTML templates are implemented varies between CMSs. Drupal, for example, requires the HTML code to be wrapped inside more complex PHP code. While the principles are straightforward, applying them can be technically daunting. Engineers are your friends.

The very first cut of your template is really just to check that everything is hooked up. It can be as simple as an HTML title tag and an H1 header displaying the First Name and Last Name attributes from the Person content type. It can be something looking approximately like this:

```
<html>
<head>
   <title>{Person: FirstName LastName}</title>
</head>
   <body>
   <h1>{Person: FirstName LastName}</h1>
   </body>
</html>
```

Associate this template with the Person content type in your CMS and publish. Shazam! Presto change-o! If everything is working, you should have resource pages for every Person record held in the CMS. Right now, they show only each person's name, and there's no navigation beyond hacking the URL in your browser bar. But you're off and running.

Next, add more attributes. Back in Chapter 7, we discussed how to design content resources by cherry-picking attributes from any of your content types. Your goal is to populate the resource with useful, relevant information based on the information-seeking needs of your visitor. From the `Person` content type, this could be

- `Name` (you already have that!)
- `Job Title`
- `Company`
- `Photo`
- `Biography`
- `Website URL`
- `Twitter ID`
- `Role`

> **NOTE** Often it's useful to incorporate information from one resource or content type within another resource, such as displaying a person's bio alongside their session. This is known as *transclusion*, a word coined by the father of connected content, Ted Nelson.

And just because this is a `Person` template doesn't mean you're limited to attributes from the `Person` content type. From other content types in the model, let's pull in

- `Event` (to show which events the person is associated with)
- `Session Title` (for any sessions the `Person` is involved with)
- `Session Time/Date`
- `Blog Title` (for any blog posts they've written)
- `Blog Date`

This supporting information adds value to the basic biography, contextualizing it to the person's involvement with one or more events. It also connects this resource type to other resources, based on the relationship between them. The HTML now looks something like the following code:

```
<html>
<head>
  <title>{Person: FirstName LastName}</title>
</head>
  <body>
  <h1>{Person: FirstName LastName}</h1>
<h2>{Person: JobTitle}</h2>
```

```
<p>{Person: Company}</p>
<p><img src="{Person: Photo}" alt="Photo of{Person: FirstName
LastName}" /></p>
<p>{Person: Biography}</p>
<a href="{Person: URL}">{Person: URL Name}</a>
<a href="https://www.twitter.com/{Person: TwitterID}">{Person:
TwitterID}</a>
<p>{Person: Role}</p>
<p>{Event: PersonID}</p>
<p>{Session: SessionName PersonID}</p>
<p>{Session: StartTime PersonID}</p>
<p>{Session: EndTime PersonID}</p>
<p>{Blog: Title PersonID}</p>
<p>{Blog: DatePublished PersonID}</p>
</body>
</html>
```

Pop that code in a web browser, and you see the super-basic template
(**FIGURE 9.2**). It's not pretty, but the content is all there in what's now a
well-structured HTML document. Reading from top to bottom, the information
is presented in an order that makes sense—name and personal details at the
top, then a biography, and finally the stuff they're doing for the event.

FIGURE 9.2 The basic
template filled with
content from the CMS.

You'll notice that the HTML includes `<h1>` and `<h2>` tags to communicate heading hierarchy and that it is shaped with HTML5 tags such as `<article>` and `<section>`. These add simple *semantics* to the HTML document, describing its structure so that a web browser knows how to display each element. Semantics also help a search engine robot, an assistive screen reader, or even a voice interface understand what each part of the document *is* and its relative importance. Just as your resources are based on a structured model, even the parts of the representation have an inherent, machine-readable order.

ADDING VISUAL STRUCTURE AND FLAIR

The document may have semantic structure, but the resources it renders are looking a little lifeless. Let's introduce visual structure to the page and make it easier for people to read. Whether for web pages, newspaper front pages, or movie posters, a logical layout establishes a visual information hierarchy that communicates meaning, connection, and importance.

Designers apply layout to an HTML document using cascading style sheets (CSS). Instructions held in CSS documents describe the presentation of elements within one or more HTML documents, keeping layout and styling cleanly separated from the content itself. CSS governs the shape and size of each element and where it should appear, either in an absolute position or relative to other elements. Those instructions may vary by device, making it possible to lay out the same HTML document differently on different devices.

Next comes styling, but let's first just take a moment and look at what you've achieved. All that work you put into research and modeling now comes together as your product takes its first breath. You have, in effect, a working skeleton of your product. It's the equivalent of the wireframe designs often mocked up early in a project. But yours are so much better than static wireframes on paper. These are powered by real content. They're alive!

This is the point at which your UX design instincts tell you that this is a great time to test your work with users. Sure, these web pages are a long way from looking finished. But as they say, always test before you think you're ready. In a usability test, you'll get valid feedback on how people engage with the actual information you propose to publish. It's so much more valuable than presenting a page of boxes and arrows and *lorem ipsum* placeholder text. Test early and often. Even with all the research and planning you've done, you won't have everything right the first time. Get real content in front of real users, real fast.

Responsive Web Design: One Size Fits All

One big advantage of considering layout and styling CSS separately from HTML document design is the ability to optimize presentation for different screen sizes. Back in 2010, designer Ethan Marcotte coined the term "responsive web design" and with it ushered in a new way of thinking about presenting HTML across multiple devices. Responsive layouts are fluid—columns have variable widths based on screen size, and content reflows accordingly. When space gets really tight, the entire layout shifts around. Multi-column layouts become single-column. Images resize. Design and content elements can even be made to appear or disappear. Done right, the whole web page appears as though perfectly designed for whatever device you're holding.

Responsive design rocks, as does Ethan's book on the subject, *Responsive Web Design* (A Book Apart, 2011). The approach focuses on presenting individual content elements on a page, so it goes just great with structured content.

Planning your responsive layout echoes the overall representation planning process described in this chapter. Figure out how you want your content to appear across each screen size you want to support. Small differences in screen width don't bring dramatic changes—the content just flexes and reflows a little bit. Eventually, though, the change in screen size causes the intended design to break. At this *breakpoint*, you need to design a new layout composed from some or all of the same pieces. (For a great example, check out Ethan Marcotte's own site: www.ethanmarcotte.com. Be sure to waggle the width of your web browser to see how the layout changes.) Responsive layouts typically include three or four breakpoints, including a mobile-friendly layout with content collapsed into a single column.

It can be tricky to figure out how the order and position of content should change across responsive breakpoints, especially the mobile breakpoint, where the single-column layout forces a very strict hierarchy. Well, tricky for some. For you it should be a breeze. Your content is already held in convenient chunks, and because you've started with an unstyled HTML document, you have a pretty good sense of how that document should be read. In fact, it's a good idea to start with this mobile view and work your way out toward a desktop design. After all, mobile devices are how most people browse the web these days.

Responsive design is a fantastic solution for serving the same HTML representation to multiple devices. Done right, your content will look great on desktop computers (of all screen resolutions), phones, tablets, and anything else that uses a modern browser. It's one of the greatest innovations in web design of the past decade, and rumor has it that Ethan now lives in a house made of gold and money. We salute you.

Once you're happy that you haven't got this whole thing horribly wrong, go ahead and continue to improve the template. CSS isn't just for layout. It also governs the visual styling of HTML documents. Typography and color. Decorative effects. Even animation. The graphic design of your resources further improves the legibility and comprehension of the content, while cementing your brand identity. Once again, there's structure and consistency here. CSS styles are associated with specific elements, such as headlines, quotations, and sidebars—all of which are defined through HTML. In fact you can define any content element you like and apply consistent styling using CSS. Again those HTML document semantics come into play. Should you need to reclassify an element (such as changing an H2 headline to an H3), the CSS makes sure that element is restyled correctly.

The designer Brad Frost has much more to say about constructing layout and styling conventions in his book *Atomic Design* (which you can read online at bradfrost.com). Brad recommends that elements be styled from the bottom up, with individual *atoms* (such as titles, form fields, and labels) combining to form molecular units (such as a login box), which themselves eventually combine in a completed template. Separating these concerns continues the approach you've taken all along. Styling is separate from layout, which is separate from document design, which is separate from content design, which is separate from the modeled domain. Splitting things out makes it easier to understand what's working and what needs revision. And when healthy creative debates spring up around styling (they always do), then at least those issues can be addressed in isolation without affecting the other parts of the system.

INDEX TEMPLATES

The same bottom-up process goes for designing your index templates. The super-basic index template is really just a list of resources. Expressing this as an HTML unordered list does the job:

```
<ul>
  <li>
    <p><img src="{Person: Photo}" alt="Photo of {Person:
FirstName LastName}" /></p>
<h2>{Person: FirstName LastName}</h2>
  </li>
</ul>
```

Lists of course, vary in length. Through CSS you control how each item in the list appears (remember the principle of proximity and keep related attributes together), and you'll also determine how that list grows or collapses dependent on the number of items it contains.

As with resource templates, well-structured HTML ensures that the list is clearly readable even without any styling applied. But with a creative choice of attribute selection and layout, lists don't have to look like lists. **FIGURE 9.3** shows the speaker page from the IA Summit site. This used the `Name` and `Picture` attributes, presenting the list as rows of smiley faces linking to their respective `Person` resource.

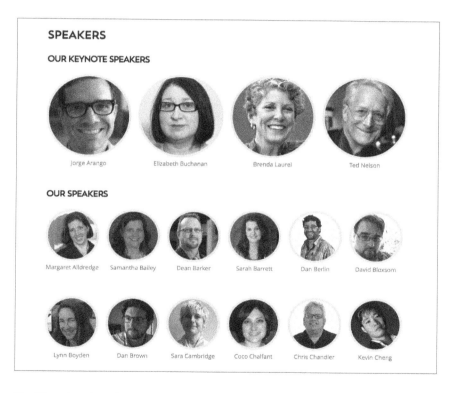

FIGURE 9.3 Detail of the IA Summit speaker index.

You'll notice that the names are shown in alphabetical order (ordered by last name). The CMS has been told to output each record in this order, made possible by the wise decision to split first and last names into separate fields. (You may recall we opened the book with a story of someone who wanted to change their last name. That change would result in the person being automatically repositioned in this alphabetical list.)

This list shows only speakers and workshop hosts. In fact, everyone involved in the event—co-chairs, curators, designers, and more—has a `Person` resource, but attendees are much more interested in knowing who'll be onstage. By limiting the list display to people with a `Role` of `Host`, we make sure only the right folks show up here. (Don't worry about the unsung heroes behind the scenes— we also built a `Team` index running from a separate template configured to display everyone who *did not* hold a `Role` of `Host`.)

You'll also notice that some people on this page are a little more equal than others. The keynote speakers are a big draw for conference attendees, so they deserve a prominent display. The template is therefore driven by two lists: one for people who hold the `Role` of `Host`, and a separate list reserved for those holding the `Keynote` role. Since it's separate, that list can be styled differently (in this case, bigger headshot photos). It also means that even if one of the keynote speakers changed their name to Zelda ZZtopperston, they'd still appear above the regular speakers.

USING INDEXES FOR CONTENT CURATION

Thinking of indexes as lists of resources is useful as a way of distinguishing them from the resources themselves, but it kinda undersells their power. The CNN.com home page is an index. The main interfaces of YouTube and Netflix are indexes. Indexes can be rich and impactful, pulling in photos, videos, and headlines from the resources they bring together. They can be built around content types, attributes of content types, or content within those attributes that matches a particular query. So they're great for pulling together a list of every car built in Italy, every conference talk on the topic of user research, or every news article published today.

Indexes can also address a common complaint of structured content—that it lacks drama. The act of chunking and homogenizing templated content resources, while perfectly consistent and logical, fails to stress the more significant examples over the long tail of also-rans. It's a fair point. In your domaindriven, non-hierarchical structure, your lemon drizzle cake recipe is exactly as important as your entry for kale salad.

Even on IMDb, the entry for *The Shawshank Redemption* is hierarchically equivalent to the entry for *Bridesmaids*. They're both instances of a `Movie` content type. Fortunately, this content type has attributes (like `Rating` and `Critic Review`) that give us insight into which is the better movie (we won't spoil it). And whenever IMDb put out a Greatest Hundred Movies list, they can use that data to determine which content resources make the cut.

So with the right content attributes determining priority, indexes can reflect a point of view. Movies by critic's score. Restaurants by cleanliness. For services like TripAdvisor and Expedia, the opinion inherent in a list's order can make or break a business.

In your business, lists may be a natural part of the culture. Soccer league tables. Bestseller lists for publishers. If the data exists, it can be attached to content types using attributes. Were we to design a bestseller aggregation for the *New York Times*, we'd probably define a content type of `Book` and include `Total Sales` among its attributes. Add a little engineering jiggery-pokery to connect the CMS to a live set of sales records, and we have the engine to power a dynamic aggregation, adjusted automatically whenever the sales figures roll in.

COLLECTIONS

Your point of view is implicit in the way you curate your content. That's good—holding the opinion that one thing is better or more significant than another establishes differentiation. It can build an audience of people who warm to your tastes. But ranking resources based on ratings will only get you so far. Consider the role of a museum or gallery curator. They don't simply shove a bunch of artworks in a room based on their similarity or importance. Instead, they hand-pick artifacts to illustrate a story. Perhaps a history of the Civil War, or advances in technology. They create a new context that gathers together things that might be otherwise unrelated.

A *collection* is a special kind of content index. Rather than items being aggregated automatically, the individual resources are hand-picked by a content author. The collection brings an editor's touch. Just as with the gallery curator and works of art, resources are chosen to fit a certain narrative. **FIGURE 9.4** shows one from the BBC Wildlife Finder.

FIGURE 9.4 A hand-curated collection of resources.

This collection features videos chosen by British naturalist David Attenborough. Each clip is an instance of a `Video` attribute in the `Individual` (animal) content type. They're described with a name, description, and thumbnail image from their respective resources. The resources still live in their original locations; the collection merely surfaces attributes from them. It brings editorial priority without breaking the structure of the underlying model.

To make a collection, you'd first define it as a content type in the CMS. Its attributes include spaces for the resources it collects, along with the collection's own name, description, photo, and whatever other descriptive properties you need. Publish the collection like any other resource, using a dedicated, reusable template.

Collections offer the chance to use your content resources to tell more stories and offer personalization without creating new content. They allow you to quickly pull together existing material into a new context. Curate content in response to current events, such as presidential elections or the worst natural disasters. Offer editorial commentary on the collection itself to contrast with the more authoritative tone taken by your main resources.

DESIGNING NAVIGATION

From menu headings on websites to tab bars on mobile apps, navigation tools (such as drop-down lists, maps, or anything that allows traversing the content) are an essential addition to your resource and index templates. They're how your visitor gets around. Your navigation design choices can lead either to an effortless glide around your product or to hopeless confusion.

All navigation is either global, contextual, or advertising.

—Tom Scott

Content navigation is often based on a taxonomic hierarchy. That is to say that the *taxonomy* (how content resources are classified and structured) is a hierarchical model of nested categories. You've probably seen hierarchical site maps that resemble a company's org chart: a home page at the top of the tree, governing a set of categories that each hold relevant content. Users drill down through increasingly specific concepts (animals > mammals > canines > dogs) until they find what they're looking for. It's the Russian nesting-doll approach to content classification. In theory, that nesting gives you a perfectly logical structure and sets up a model fit for future expansion. In practice, information is messy and often resists the constraints of hierarchy. The platypus is both mammal and reptile. The single-celled organism *Euglena* has characteristics of both plants and animals. RoboCop is part man, part machine (and all cop). Whatever hierarchy you design, you'll undoubtedly encounter content examples that refuse to sit comfortably within a single branch.

MODEL-BASED NAVIGATION

With your modeling work, you've taken a different approach. Rather than sorting content into specific buckets, you've analyzed the concepts inherent to that content and figured out how they fit together. You've already untangled the complexities of the domain and developed a vocabulary of terms that make sense to your audience. You already have your taxonomy, and this structure is far richer and closer to reflecting reality than a simple hierarchy could hope to be. Now through a system of global and contextual navigation, you'll bring it to the surface.

GLOBAL NAVIGATION

Global navigation is literally everywhere in your product. It's your main menu of navigational choices, and it doesn't change or move around as you travel. Global navigation is an important aid to usability. It helps a visitor immediately establish an overall context, seeing at a glance the kinds of information you have to offer. As they explore, global navigation lets them know broadly where they are and offers a way out. No matter how hopelessly lost they become, the global navigation will get them back to safety. It's their fire escape out of your structure and their teleport between the principal realms of your product.

CONTEXTUAL NAVIGATION

As the name suggests, contextual navigation provides supporting context. The navigation tools are focused on a specific area. For example, the Clothing, Shoes & Jewelry section of Amazon has quite different navigation options than the Home & Kitchen section. Like its global counterpart, contextual navigation can serve as a way of establishing what's available. It also helps a visitor understand how a content resource relates to the overall domain. Should visitors arrive at the content resource directly from their Google results, the visible navigation helps them figure out what they're looking at. Contextual navigation can also be applied to the content itself. It's common in feature articles to add inline links as cross-references to people, news events, or previous reports. In some cases, inline links can become the dominant mode of navigation (hello again, Wikipedia).

Together, global and contextual navigation (**FIGURES 9.5** and **9.6**) form the bridges between your content resources. Navigation shows your visitor how you think the subject domain is structured. It exposes your point of view.

BUILDING THE FIRE ESCAPE

Global navigation provides the inroads to your main content areas. Luckily, you've already spent an almost indecent amount of time defining what these areas are. Design your global navigation around your core content types and you provide direct access to the things your visitors most want to find.

The BBC's redesign of their *Food* website began with a domain model, capturing what research uncovered as the most important concepts. Recipes, TV chefs, ingredients, cookery techniques, and the BBC's own cooking shows map the territory. **FIGURE 9.7** shows what we find in the global navigation—why, it's those self-same domain objects!

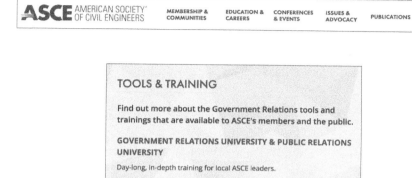

FIGURE 9.5 Global navigation remains in place wherever you go.

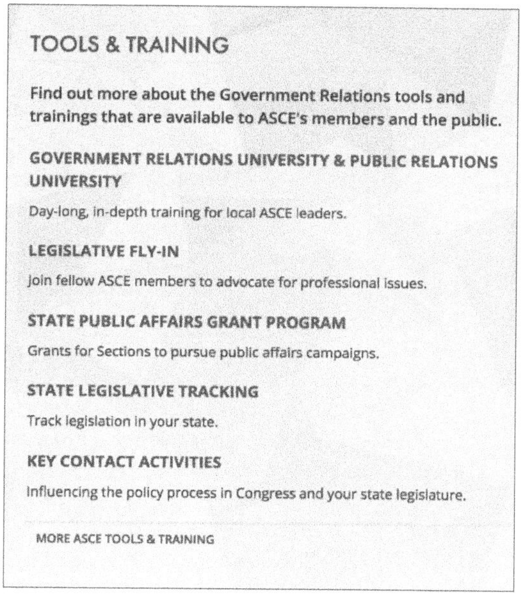

FIGURE 9.6 Contextual navigation is scoped to a specific area.

FIGURE 9.7 A global navigation based on domain objects.

Each menu option links to an aggregation of resources for the appropriate content type.

In the Ingredients index (**FIGURE 9.8**), `Name` and `Photo` attributes from the `Ingredient` content type link to resources for each instance.

FIGURE 9.8 An index comprising the **Name** and **Photo** attributes of the **Ingredient** content type.

> **NOTE** Sometimes you'll want additional menu items in your navigation (maybe Contact or About Us) that aren't necessarily content types. That's fine—your global navigation doesn't have to be exclusively content types. Just make sure the main ones are present and correct.

For the IA Summit website, we faced a navigational dilemma. The multi-event model needed a structure that placed the upcoming event as merely one instance of the overall event brand. Yet to a visitor, the information about that specific event was of primary importance. The template design (**FIGURE 9.9**) helped supply the right emphasis, while the truly global navigation was about the event brand (and therefore limited to things outside any one event, like general information about the event and sponsorship opportunities). The visual impact of the event-specific navigation made this the focus of the page.

FIGURE 9.9 Global navigation balanced with event-specific navigation.

Again, the navigation for the event-specific information is built around content types:

- **Speakers:** An index of people who hold the role of Host or Keynote

- **Schedule:** An index of sessions, sorted chronologically by the CMS

- **Minneapolis:** A specific blog post that detailed the local area

- **Team 2015:** An index of people who did not hold the role of Host or Keynote

- **Blog:** An index of posts from the content type Blog Post

Placed above these are links to resources about the conference brand overall. These aren't specific to the 2015 event, so they are positioned to communicate their higher order in the conceptual hierarchy.

LEARNING THROUGH THE LINKS

Speaking of sidebars, contextual navigation is where you get to make good on all those theoretical connections you modeled. As with our beloved *Top Trumps* game, your content attributes offer interesting facts that support the main content. That additional context can even teach the visitor a little more about the subject of the resource than is implicit in the content alone.

FIGURE 9.10 shows the sidebar infobox from a Wikipedia article. The information is presented as a factual summary, but it serves as contextual navigation. It's useful information by itself, made all the more useful by connecting to other resources. This opens up journeys of discovery based on the inherent connections between concepts. It's learning through linking.

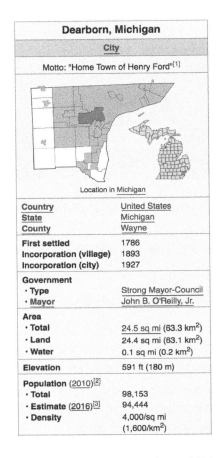

In Chapter 7, we mentioned that there's no need to publish content for your entire model all at once. You may have modeled the concept of a sports car's designer, but you're waiting on biographies to be researched and archive interview footage to be cleared. It's no problem—you know each designer's name, so you can fill out that information in the CMS. That would be enough to associate Sergio Pininfarina with your Ferrari Testarossa resource. But perhaps you've delayed publishing resources for each designer until you have some decent content available. That's fine. Your `Vehicle` resource template can still show the `Designer` attribute. It just won't be linked until the relevant `Designer` resources are published.

MY NAME IS URL

We saved the most important kind of navigation for last, although really it's the one you should be planning from the start. URL (uniform resource locator) design is perhaps the most often overlooked part of designing for the web, but creating a logical arrangement of access to your material is a fundamental part of the experience.

URLs are web addresses. Things like

- http://www.nasa.gov
- http://www.theguardian.com/film
- http://www.nytimes.com/science

Design your URLs around your principal content types because these represent the real-world people, places, and things that people want to access. If you have a content type of `Person`, then make your URL something like:

http://www.example.com/people

You could opt for the singular /person if you prefer, but it's reasonable to expect that this address would connect to an index of all your `Person` records. Similarly, if you had an index of all conference events (based on an `Event` content type) you'd want a URL of:

http://www.example.com/events

You'd therefore expect the resource for a specific event to be found at:

http://www.example.com/events/specific_event

Make sense so far? Well what if you wanted to know all the people who were associated with a specific event? Probably not the www.example.com/people URL above, since that doesn't carry any information about a specific event (and might return a list of all people for all events ever). So for people in a single event, try:

http://www.example.com/events/specific_event/people

Sure it's getting long, but it accurately reflects the information retrieved. It's also what the cool kids call *hackable*—at every backslash there's some valuable content to be found. We'd expect this URL to return a list of all people associated with the event, in whatever capacity. But what if you only wanted to see the speakers? Maybe you'd go to:

http://www.example.com/events/specific_event/people/speakers

Here you'd offer an index restricted to people who held a particular role. Yes, the URL is getting super-long, but we'll deal with that later. So far this may all seem pretty straightforward and hierarchical. You're drilling down from a broad concept to a specific instance of that concept, and then to detailed information scoped to that instance. But so far all these URLs reference only indexes. What if you wanted to address the resource for a particular speaker within the specific event? The URL may surprise you:

http://www.example.com/people/:person

So there are a couple of things to unpack here. First off, why isn't it events/specific_event/speakers/:person? You'll recall from our tales of the IA Summit that we designed with the future in mind. A person might be associated with one or more events, but they're always the same person. And if we think of URLs as addressing a digital stand-in for an actual person, then it would be wrong to define that person in terms of that one time they did a talk at an event. Each person's record in the CMS chronicles their involvement in each event, but that context doesn't need to be baked into the URL itself.

Second, what's with that colon on :person? Of course, to be addressed individually, each person gets their own unique URL. Since the "person" bit on the end is the only part that changes, the colon is a notation convention that says "put the actual reference here."

Referencing resources in URLs can be tricky. People often expect a lovely human-readable reference, something posh like:

http://www.example.com/people/victoria_adams

But when Miss Adams becomes Mrs. Victoria Beckham, a little part of the internet breaks. The URL is no longer accurate, but changing it destroys any links, bookmarks, or even search results associated with it. Web inventor Tim Berners-Lee once said, "Cool URLs don't change." The addresses you maintain for your content resources serve as a promise to those who visit you, bookmark you, or reference you in their own work. Messing around with your URLs would be like moving house without telling your friends (let's assume that's a bad thing). Persistence is therefore perhaps the most important factor in URL design. That means avoiding anything within the URL that's subject to change. Things like names of people, places, or article titles (where that title becomes part of the URL itself) are all a little fragile. A drastic yet effective approach is to do away with proper resource names altogether and instead use IDs, as with:

http://www.bbc.co.uk/programmes/b00jnwnv

This URL points to a resource for the US drama *The Wire*, a show that is occasionally rerun on various BBC broadcast and digital channels. It doesn't make sense to include any channel information in the URL, since the show may appear on many different channels at some point between now and the end of time. And curiously in this case, the name *The Wire* is shared by a couple of unrelated radio documentaries. All these shows are available in the BBC's online archive, so using the "b00jnwnv" unique ID makes it clear which *The Wire* to aim at.

Unique IDs take some of the pain out of planning for persistence. They disambiguate resources, avoiding confusion over things with similar names. They remain unaltered even when the name of the resource they point to changes. They're not exactly elegant, although many would argue they're meant for the computer and not for humans at all. But still, if you want to read an address out over the radio or put an ad on the side of a bus, you really don't want something full of backslashes and ending in a string of gobbledygook.

That's when the humble 301 redirect can help. You're probably familiar with HTTP status code 404, which confronts you when the page you're looking for can't be found. The 301 is its more helpful cousin that tells the computer that a resource has moved permanently to another location. When you request a document that's been moved elsewhere, the web server bounces you to the updated location. Using this feature for nefarious (or rather, marketing) purposes allows you to promote a "vanity" address, such as bbc.co.uk/sherlock, which when entered redirects to:

http://www.bbc.co.uk/programmes/b018ttws

Once you arrive, the site design and navigation capture your attention. Most people don't notice the switch of address at all. Redirects are a trick best done sparingly, however—too many and you'll find your links falling down the Google rankings.

URI Teller

Read about this stuff elsewhere and you might see the term URI (uniform resource identifier) rather than URL. A URI identifies a content resource by name (albeit a name such as "example.com/resource"), and a URL tells the computer where that resource can be found, including its internet protocol—that's the "http://" part, although other fine protocols are available. Make sense? Thought not. The two terms have long caused confusion, and the distinction between them is subtle. In fact a URL is a type of URI, but not the other way around. Your concern is designing logical pathways to resources, so let's keep things simple for now and stick with URL.

Even if you're not intent on making a website, URL design is crucial. All your content is delivered over the web, even when represented through a mobile app or a Siri response. The same URL structure is used to serve the content to all representations, even those never seen by a human, so maintain sensible conventions that keep everything working now and in the future.

BEING EVERYWHERE

We've talked a lot about web pages, but what if your goal is a mobile app? Squint a bit, and the process looks pretty similar. Your content is still stored and structured within a CMS. We've just walked through a process for designing human-friendly HTML representations of your resources. But those resources can be represented in other ways, including machine-readable data.

Smartphone apps are written using custom frameworks or languages. iOS apps are developed using a language named Swift. Android apps use the Java-based Android SDK. While your CMS can't be expected to publish Swift or Android representations with the same ease as it does HTML, what it can do is respond to requests made by the app and return structured content in a format the app understands and can display. This is commonly done through a *content API* (application programming interface), which is a means for two computers to connect and share information.

Content APIs are a standard feature of some CMS platforms. Often, though, engineers will develop their own custom extensions to an existing platform.

Depending on requirements and capabilities, that API may send content to the requesting application either as binary data or in a structured format such as JSON.

JSON (JavaScript Object Notation) is a popular file format for supplying structured information to applications. Its notation style (shown in the following code) is fairly straightforward to make sense of, even for a human. To represent a content resource, the JSON file includes attribute names along with the values of those attributes. Unlike HTML, it doesn't include anything about document presentation, such as `<title>` or `<h1>` tags. Instead, the responsibility for how to present the content is governed by the receiving application. JSON's notation style looks like this:

```
{
"firstName": "Paul",
"lastName": "Rissen",
"isAlive": true,

"job": {
"jobTitle": "Product Manager",
"employer": "Springer Nature",

},
"session":
{
"sessionName": "Designing Webs -  IA as a Creative Practice",
"sessionStart": "2015-04-25T16:00:00-07:00"
"sessionEnd": "2015-04-25T16:45:00-07:00"
},
}
```

The application typically requests a complete JSON document for a particular resource. The app designer is then free to present some or all of this content through their interface. JSON representations are used to supply content to everything from Android apps to Amazon Echo skills. When you ask Alexa "Wikipedia Snow Leopard," that's a JSON file she's reading.

By using a content API, your CMS can serve representations to any web, mobile, tablet, or smartwatch app you create. And even the ones you don't. In Chapter 2, we commented on the technological and behavioral shift in how and where we get our content. These days, it wouldn't be unusual for people to access your resources without ever visiting your website or app at all. Facebook Instant Articles and Google AMP pages are increasingly popular, albeit controversial, platforms for content publishing. They offer the potential to put content in front of a lot more people. And all you need to be there is a specially formatted HTML representation of your content.

For the brave and the bold, the content API can unlock crowdsourced content distribution. License your material for redistribution (such as under a Creative Commons license), and allow third parties to request API access. Publish machine-readable representations publicly (**FIGURE 9.11**). Let other people use your content to drive their innovation (hopefully with attribution back to you, but even that's negotiable). Make it easy for app developers to incorporate your specialist and authoritative content, and you're on your way to becoming the *de facto* standard in your field. When we think maps, we think Google Maps. Movie info and ratings? IMDb. General-knowledge encyclopedic content? Who else but Wikipedia? Content syndication at the API level might seem overly generous, but it drives growth. It puts your content in more places than you could ever hope to reach by yourself. Such a strategy has helped publishers like IMDb, Google, and Wikipedia make their content, and their brand, more or less ubiquitous.

```
– <rdf:RDF>
  – <rdf:Description rdf:about="/nature/species/Giant_Panda">
      <foaf:primaryTopic rdf:resource="/nature/species/Giant_Panda#species"/>
      <rdfs:seeAlso rdf:resource="/nature/species/"/>
  </rdf:Description>
  – <wo:Species rdf:about="/nature/life/Giant_Panda#species">
      <rdfs:label>Giant panda</rdfs:label>
      <wo:name rdf:resource="http://www.bbc.co.uk/nature/species/Giant_Panda#name"/>
      <foaf:depiction rdf:resource="http://ichef.bbci.co.uk/naturelibrary/images/ic/640x360/g/gi/giant_panda/giant_panda_1.jpg"/>
    – <dc:description>
      The giant panda is a rare, endangered and elusive
      <a href="http://www.bbc.co.uk/nature/life/Bear">bear</a>
      , making the videos below of a newborn baby giant panda and the remarkable courtship scene filmed in the wild unique. Giant
      pandas are famous for their love of bamboo, a diet so nutritionally poor that the pandas have to consume up to 20kg each day. The
      extra digit on the panda's hand helps them to tear the bamboo and their gut is covered with a thick layer of mucus to protect against
      splinters. Habitat loss is the greatest cause of the giant panda's decline, and today their range is restricted to six separate mountain
      ranges in western
      <a href="http://www.bbc.co.uk/nature/places/China">China</a>
```

FIGURE 9.11 Wildlife Finder offers machine-readable representations of its resources.

STABLE STRUCTURE, CREATIVE CONTENT

Even the most compelling content benefits from well-designed presentation, and there's no reason why a reusable template can't be as visually rich, interactive, and exciting as something crafted entirely by hand. It just takes a little forethought. Thankfully, you have forethought to spare. Fivethought even. By planning content in advance, you know which kinds of resources you want to publish and which chunks make up each resource. That's a big help in knowing which interface templates to create. Through your connected structure, you've defined the principal concepts within your domain and the relationships between them. That means you've pretty much nailed your navigation.

Separating content and structure from presentation lets you keep your interface options open. A humble index list can be transformed into a map or an interactive timeline. Global navigation can be improved and expanded, providing access to new indexes based on content attributes. Maybe it turns out that people are really interested in those sports car designers, and `Designers` deserves a spot in the main menu.

Always consider context. The factors surrounding your audience's use of your product should drive the content you offer and the way it's presented. Where and when are they using your product? Comfortably at home, or alone on a street late at night? What information do they need most often? Is it easy to find in a hurry? Even their emotional state should affect your design decisions. An emergency number for people who've been in a car accident should not be buried three levels deep in a slow and complicated website that isn't mobile-friendly.

Each representation can remix content types and attributes to offer a new take on your content, appropriate for different contexts. Low-bandwidth versions. Accessible versions. Even content delivered to older technology such as feature phones, still popular in emerging markets. With structured content, it's relatively easy to experiment with different modes of presentation. And as new devices come along, supporting them may be as straightforward as building a lightweight application powered by JSON representations from your CMS. Content is your design material, and, dependent on device, that material can be stitched together any way you choose.

LOOKING BACK

Through the last few chapters, we've taken you through a process we've learned over time. It's not an exact science, and while we've tried to present things step by step, chances are you won't follow it to the letter. And that's okay—every situation is different. Every CMS, doubly so. More important is the guiding philosophy behind it: to structure and create your content based on the mental models of your audience *before* you start to represent it through an interface. Because user experience design isn't limited to the user interface. The overall experience is the ability to find, consume, and make sense of your content whenever your audience needs it and wherever they are. While it's important to get the interface right, the most fundamental value lies under the surface.

It's almost time to go. Before we look to the future, thank you for indulging our procedural complexity. If this process is working for you, or if it's really not, let us know. Find us on Twitter. We're @carriehd and @mikeatherton, and we'd love to hear from you.

Now turn around and see how far you've come. You've designed and built a digital product not just for today, but for tomorrow. And probably the day after that. The future, basically.

THE FUTURE

CHAPTER 10

THE FUTURE ISN'T WAITING

The world keeps moving. Voice user interfaces have found their way into our everyday lives. Artificial intelligence is on the table, and not only in the boardroom. In the United Nations, global leaders discuss potential regulation of AI and propose limits on its application. The screens we've long stared at are beginning to disappear.

Throughout this book, we've tried to celebrate a process that can bring your content to all kinds of technology, but not wanting to get too wrapped up in examples of the tech *du jour*. The principles of connected content apply to any current technology and help you get ready for whatever comes next.

When we talk about a screenless world, we don't just mean the Amazon Echo and its cousins. We mean a world where the main job of each publisher is creating and connecting content, because the interfaces mostly lie elsewhere or are owned by other providers. This new frontier will be won by those with content of quality and distinction. But the shift to content-first isn't just about changing workflow, it's also about changing minds.

REAL TALK

Prepare yourself for a plot twist. We haven't been entirely honest with you. When writing a book like this, it's tempting to make the whole process seem like smooth sailing. You want a success story, a result you too can achieve with our simple five-step weight loss plan! But when we tell you a story of how we managed near-perpetual future stability for an organization's digital content, evidence to the contrary is only a Google search away.

If you visit the IA Summit website today, you won't see our work. You won't see structured content resources connecting the people and sessions of today to the events of the past. Instead you'll see an entirely new one-off website, built on a new platform by a new team. What happened?

Content management can be scary, but sometimes it's the place we run to when people management looks scarier. We convinced our event committee on the on the structured content approach, but our mistake was to leave it at that. Once that team left office, the project was undefended. The institutional knowledge drained away, replaced by the energy and ideas of a new team eager to make their own mark.

And to be honest, our IA Summit website didn't look especially impressive. With limited time and resources available, we chose to invest in the underlying structure. But, of course, visitors judged it on the impact of its interface and found it lacking. The power and potential of structured content becomes more apparent over time, yet we offered information limited to the 2015 event. And we represented those resources through templates completed in too much of a hurry. Despite what fine machinery may purr under the hood, to the casual observer it looked an awful lot like the one-off websites they knew. Only a little bit worse. We were guilty of seeing what it would and could be rather than what it was. Where we saw the foundations of a content cathedral, others saw a construction site. No one outside the project committee knew what we were trying to do.

It's not all bad news. A volunteer collective still beavers away to, um, squirrel away the slides, audio and video recordings, transcripts, photos, and other valuable artifacts from every IA Summit session. With a bit of digging, they even discovered some ancient history: the HTML pages for IA Summit events dating back to 2000. These relics lay forgotten on a network drive. The pages themselves haven't aged well, but embedded within them are the best known records of each session. That might not mean a whole lot to you, but to an information architect it's like unearthing the original flyer for the Sermon on the Mount. Kinda.

As long as all this content exists, all is not lost. In its original form it may lack structure, but that's easy enough to add, even if it means copying and pasting text into a modern CMS. And the modeling work has gone a long way to translate the complexities and quirks of the domain into blueprints for content types and interface templates. For now it will lie in pieces on the garage floor, like a sports car restoration project that begs to be completed.

Other conferences have borrowed our domain model to kickstart their own work. That's the beauty of a domain model—it's intended to be reusable. Along the way we included some relationships that may apply only to our use case, but they're not too hard to adapt. When you model a subject domain, you attempt to prioritize and capture the things that are most true, most often. That can result in a model that naturally reflects every example of that domain—every conference, every theme park, every sports car—giving it value beyond the examples you'll cover. If every business in the same industry worked from a common model of that industry, "connected content" could ascend to a whole new level. But more on that in a little bit.

ORGANIZATIONAL CULTURE

Addressing content concerns is really the easier of your two challenges. The harder one is addressing your organization's culture. Experience has taught us that building for the future isn't just about technology. It's about people. It's about putting in place the long-term commitment and executive sponsorship to protect your project even as things change. Short-term thinking is your biggest obstacle. Building for the future sets you up for steady product growth and evolution. But often product managers and stakeholders seek drastic revolutions that show conspicuous change. A project with tightly defined edges and a newsworthy launch can seem more attractive than something that involves building a lot of invisible structure and that relies on ongoing governance.

Even Tom Scott's fabulous BBC Wildlife Finder couldn't survive without a governance plan and executive sponsorship. That site is still up and working, but visit bbc.co.uk/nature/animals and the imposing sign overhead reads "last updated October 2014." The product's elegant content structure fizzes with timeless television clips, but the interface already shows its age, and, for now it seems, this natural world's evolution has come to a stop. When Tom left the BBC, Wildlife Finder lost its champion.

Your digital strategy is itself a representation of the will of your organization to deliver the right content to the right people at the right time. And where's there's a will, designing connected content is a way forward.

Throughout this book, we've made the case that using structured content is a better investment of time and resources than the endless cycle of redesign. But it's a brave and insightful business owner who recognizes this pattern of behavior and is prepared to break it. More commonly they're like yo-yo dieters. There comes a point in a website's life where everyone finally admits that things have gotten too heavy. The instinct is to jettison everything and start again, in the hope that a "clean design" will make for a more lightweight experience. Purging can be good. Taking the opportunity to flush out all the redundant, outdated, and trivial content is definitely a positive step. But as with physical weight loss, sustainable results are possible only when you change your mindset. And yet, after the launch of the sleek new website, more and more content gets added back. Stakeholder requests creep in. Each piece of content and each new feature add a couple of pounds here, a couple of pounds there. And then you're back to where you started.

Your content is *about* your business, not *for* your business. Your digital channels are not a magazine where each business department writes and publishes its own section independently. Instead, your digital strategy must present a cohesive whole designed around the needs of your audience and intended to meet those needs as efficiently as possible. Though, as we've mentioned before, those launch-hungry stakeholders can still get their glory when they commission interface representations that bring a new window to the same world of structured content beneath. And well they should—to paraphrase an old tech saying, interfaces age like fish, but content ages like wine.

CONVINCING YOUR BOSS

So how do you get the powers that be to play ball? Start by buying them all a copy of this book. And maybe a spare copy for the weekend. But speaking of revenue generation (ours), the real answer is of course to hit them in the wallet.

What matters most to the person holding the purse strings? What's important to you or your team may not be top priority for your boss or your boss's boss. For many, it's simply about making money or saving money. For others, it's about leaving a legacy or delivering on a long-promised strategy. We've covered these arguments before, but here they are once more as you prep for that meeting. They've worked for us.

- **Make the most of the content you already have.** Buried in the rock face of your website are some real content gems. Give them a chance to shine. You're not proposing massive amounts of content creation or completely changing the corporate message. You're just proposing to get the inventory in good shape for whatever comes next. By adding structure, you're allowing the content that's already been paid for to be reused more easily across channels. You're doing more with less.

- **Point your limited production resources toward what's most useful.** By starting your content planning with user needs, you're focusing effort on the most useful content for your audience. Instead of falling into the trap of producing more and more expensive content, you're making smart choices about the right content. Stop wasting time and money on vanity content or products that don't meet a defined objective. Instead, align your digital strategy with your business strategy.

- **Avoid expensive and time-consuming redesigns.** No matter how much you want to plan and model and generally try to lasso the future, things will change. Structured content embraces that change, providing a stable foundation on which to build and expand. This could be the last complete website or app redesign you ever have to do. Structured content projects don't necessarily cost any more than building one-off large products, but they deliver value for much longer. And maintaining them will be cheaper over time because they're easier to keep updated, easier to visually refresh, and easier to scale without getting messy. Not a bad return on investment.

- **Lower risk and improve customer service.** Losing duplicate content lowers the risk of having inaccurate information out there, which can only improve your customer experience. Have you ever had to give a customer a lower price because an update didn't happen in the one place that everyone forgot about? What happens when old information on a page that is no longer maintained gets quoted in the press? It is better to produce focused resources that keep all the content on a topic in a single place. There's just one place to keep track of, with those updates reflected everywhere. Less content to manage means more time to spend on improving customer satisfaction.

- **Be everywhere.** Google, Facebook, Twitter, PubMed, refrigerators, watches, phones, cars. Be wherever your audience is. That's not going to happen if you have to maintain content separately for each channel or device. Structure sets your content free and allows you to be in more places at once while staying in control of your content and, with it, your brand. Extend your reach without the expense.

MAKING THIS HAPPEN

Selling anything is difficult. It's even more difficult when someone isn't looking to buy. So for all the reasoned arguments, you may be more effective doing good deeds by stealth. Larger organizations can be monuments to bureaucracy and inertia. But they're also big enough to hide in. Think about making a structured content prototype, *Ocean's Eleven* style. Form a crew of engineers, designers, and content authors. A rebel alliance. A coalition of the willing. Under the guise of research or a small website build, try doing things the connected content way. Try it even if it means using a different CMS or hacking together some version of your own. After all, when was the last time a senior stakeholder cared which system was serving up their website?

Don't overdo it, though; choose a small part of the domain to focus on. The goal is a proof-of-concept demo that shows how easily content can be created centrally and pushed into nicely designed, interlinked templates across different devices. Rather than going to your boss with arguments you got from a book, you're offering proof that this is a good idea and, more importantly, that you're able to pull it together. Maybe that all sounds a little maverick, but some great digital projects have been born from committed teams working outside the rules and asking for forgiveness, not permission.

Even if you have a greenlight from the get-go, starting small is still a good idea. Your team hasn't worked this way before, so getting from start to finish quickly helps them buy into the approach. If your domain is complex, then those first steps of modeling can be tough. You're asking for a lot of abstract thinking from people who don't yet see the payoff. Start with a small section that everyone understands and carry that all the way through. Even if you don't end up with something you want to launch publicly, you'll have taken your team on the structured content journey. You will make mistakes. But when you do, having distinct layers of structure baked into your product will help you zero in on the parts that need attention later. When layers are created with care, any layer can be adjusted or expanded at any time.

As a team, you'll build common ground with the insights you gain together. As you continue to expand your model, you'll add more content types and attributes to accommodate new service lines or business functions. It's a framework. It's one that adapts to new requirements, audiences, or business objectives. And before you know it, your small project will become a big project as you start to merge those old microsites and PDF black holes into a single, extensible network of knowledge.

MEASURING SUCCESS

Put away your perfectionist tendencies. Done is better than perfect. Move fast. Be bold. Just get your content out there already! That's the only way to know if something is working. Don't get mired in getting the model just right or the CMS set up just so for each and every author. But do agree on measurable goals to set a direction and know when you need to change course. Content strategy's output may be content, but it's the *strategy* that gets it there, makes it right, and keeps it coming. Success doesn't always travel in a straight line. Let your model be your map.

"If it doesn't ship, it doesn't count."

Focus on providing useful and usable content for your audience. Adding structure makes content easier to find and make sense of. You'll see evidence of success in your search logs, analytics, and user research. Organic search traffic goes up for new keywords. Conversions (however you've defined them) increase. Pathfinding reports show people reaching their destination in fewer steps. Related resources see more concentrated traffic. Usability testing shows that task completion rates are high and effort expended is low. And you drink from the keg of glory.

Well, hopefully. Sometimes things don't go as planned, but you can't move what you don't measure. Don't be afraid to unpublish content or try a new way of presenting it. Remember that new representations are less of a headache when the content structure is firmly in place.

It's not just about your content. Take a look at your team too. Rework parts of the process so you're getting the right inputs and outputs. There is no right or wrong. Continuous and incremental improvement is success.

IT'S JUST INFORMATION ARCHITECTURE

We couldn't really tell the story of an IA conference without acknowledging that when we talk about content structure, domain models, and the like, we're really talking about information architecture. As a job, "information architect" sadly sounds like a dusty relic of the 1990s. It lost its cool with the rise of the UX designer, the technological shift toward lightweight mobile app structures, and, arguably, a cultural shift away from the web as a direct publishing channel and toward "products," many of which are really spaces for users to store and share content of their own.

If you're reading this, your organization is probably joining industries that have traditionally published content at scale for generations: media, government, a society or professional association, or a large corporate body bogged down by knowledge bases. And it's a safe bet you don't have a card-carrying information architect on staff. If you do, send them the finest muffins and bagels in the land. They're lonely. And if that's you, we wrote this book to help you show people why you matter. And we share your pain when people call it "AI."

All this stuff is just information architecture. It's been around for years in one form or another. Dan Klyn, information architect and co-founder of the Understanding Group, proposes a model for the discipline, dividing it into three interdependent parts:

- **Ontology:** Defining the terms that exist within the bounds of a domain with the understanding that the definitions themselves are probably specific to the domain. "Goal" means something very different to a soccer player than it does to a project manager.

- **Taxonomy:** Arranging terms based on the relationships between them in order to help people make sense of the overall domain.

- **Choreography:** The rules for how and when information held in the taxonomic structure should be presented. This includes navigation tools and the choices we make about which content to show in different channels to craft a particular experience.

Mastering these elements is the key to creating products that help people find content and make sense of it. Whenever an app or website leads us down a blind alley, makes us feel lost, or generally causes us confusion, we're apt to dismiss it as "bad UX." But the root cause of that symptom is bad information architecture. And that, more than anything, is why we urge you to avoid the temptation to start your projects by designing interface mockups; focus instead on what lies beneath.

LINKING DATA

We promised to return to the heady possibilities of a world where everyone publishing content about the same domain conforms to the same domain model. That world has yet to become mainstream, but as sci-fi author William Gibson said, "The future is already here. It's just not evenly distributed."

Back in Chapter 1 we made the rude claim that "content is data." That within any given article, blog post, or video clip lie references to *things*—specific people, places, and concepts. And that it's our interest in the *things* that draw us toward the content about them. This revelation first came to web inventor Tim Berners-Lee not long after unleashing his infernal contraption on the world. The web was great at connecting documents together; what if we could connect the data inside them? His motivations were academic. University labs sharing their genome research through open standards. Treating the web as one big database—machine-readable records that could be queried, cross-referenced, and computed as easily as the stuff sitting on your own servers. But the potential for linked data doesn't lie only in the lab.

What if every time you mentioned "Prince," you could tell the computer you meant the singer Prince Rogers Nelson and were making no claims about constitutional monarchy? And what if all other publishers did the same? Suddenly web searches could get a lot more accurate; rather than matching keywords, they could be matching meaning. Or what if whenever you published the contact details of a branch office, you could automatically pull in a Google map of the location? Or temporarily fill gaps in your resources with content from Wikipedia? What if, recognizing that people now get their movie showtimes directly from other services, you wanted to make sure your independent cinema was listed among them?

There's a whole other book that someone should write on using linked data in content strategy, and we hesitate to even puncture this can of delicious worms. Suffice it to say that connecting your own content is only the beginning. Real connectivity comes by connecting at "web scale," using common reference points to define and disambiguate resources so that every piece of content from every publisher can express the things it references in a way that computers can understand and connect. With the right metadata, you can describe your content using terms from common vocabularies. Schema.org is the best place to start. And, true to our principles, rather than replicate their guidance here, consider this a link to their content.

WHAT'S NEXT?

In the 1980s, architect Buckminster Fuller developed the idea of a "knowledge doubling curve." Until the 20th century, human knowledge doubled every 100 years. By 1945 it was every 25 years. Now, thanks in large part to the invention of the world wide web, it's estimated to be every 13 months and on track to be a matter of hours. In 2010, 24 hours of video were uploaded to YouTube every minute. Now it's 400 hours every minute.

Not so long ago, computers were all warbling modems and 80-column text displays, tainting the air with burning dust and possibility. Now they're impossibly sophisticated pocket devices, connecting us instantly to everyone we know and to that exponential growth in human knowledge. It's a curious thing; as the technology becomes more advanced, it starts to disappear. We look straight through that little glass window toward the people and places on the other side.

Trends in interface design continue to evolve. The lickable acid-colored candy of the "Web 2.0" era gave way to high-fidelity skeuomorphic realism. Then there was the minimalist "flat design" trend, sparked by the need for more responsive, CSS-driven interfaces. Hot new devices launch with a fanfare, predicted to disrupt everything and kill off their predecessors. But radio didn't kill newspapers, and television didn't kill radio. So although voice skills and chatbots and virtual reality all offer thrilling possibilities, they will find their place alongside websites and apps and even email.

Even people's expectations change, as technology ushers in behavioral shifts. Personalized curation, inherent to the experience of Amazon or Facebook, attempts to show us news stories, products, or advertising based on our past actions. That content drives engagement, in part because it's in the path of least resistance. We get the content we want, right there in our Facebook feed. Intelligent agents like Google Now monitor our email and web searches and proactively serve up relevant information at the moment we need it most. The ethical considerations of all this are complex, but one thing is clear: More and more, people expect the right content to *come to them* at the right time.

Change is the only constant. The details of the devices don't matter. Interfaces are a means to an end. If we can chart any future trend from observing the past, it's that interfaces and devices are becoming increasingly ephemeral. Invisible. We're tending toward pure content delivery. Separated from the silo of the website, and even from any controllable form of representation, your content will compete on quality and distinctiveness. From an entire web of knowledge, we'll get the most relevant information sent through the least resistive means. If this were sci-fi, it would be jacked directly into our brains. Right now we'll have to make do with chatting to Siri and Alexa.

"God grant me the serenity to accept the things I cannot change, courage to change the things I can, and wisdom to know the difference."

—*Reinhold Niebuhr*

Personalization and ubiquity will shape the future of content strategy. Your content has to be ready to be everywhere and delivered with precision to the people it's meant for. "Everywhere'" requires content unbound by interface containers. Personalization requires content broken into tightly focused chunks, its topical categories readable by people and machines. Structured content is a solid implementation tactic, but the strategy driving it is up to you. The tactics won't take hold until a system of belief is in place.

We're optimistic about the future of digital content and about the evolving mindset of those who create it. Ted Nelson, the father of hypertext, wrote in 1974 that "everything is deeply intertwingled." It's a notion held by all who've attempted to tame the roots and branches of knowledge. Eventually, we realize there are no clear borders between subjects, topics, or domains. It's one universe. Connections in our content simply represent how the world joins up.

All this talk of multichannel personalization can sound overwhelming, but you really can go a long way without much effort. Just design your content to be more connected, and let the computers take care of the rest. And if you can't get your organization to commit to big changes, start with small ones that map to business objectives. With technology and with people, success comes from making the right connections and, sometimes, just knowing which buttons to push.

INDEX

Numbers & symbols

1:1 relationships, 81
1:*n* relationships, 81, 82–83
m:n relationships, 81–83

A

Advisory Board, 27
Agile development, 63
Amazon Echo, 186, 195, 201
Andrews, Michael, 42
Association for Information Science & Technology (ASIS&T), 15
Atomic Design (Frost), 180
atoms, 180
attributes
　adding to HTML resource template, 176
　auditing content mapping to, 133
　context for defining, 106
　defined, 33, 104
　defining content type, 103–106
　determining range of, 104
　developing template from content model, 128–132
　domain object, 107
　of domain objects, 77–78, 79
　including data types for CMS field specs, 152–154
audience
　considering usefulness to, 77
　providing content for, 24, 119
　relevance of domain objects to, 100
auditing content, 132–133, 137
authors
　contacting book's, 198
　structuring content, 148–149
　using content spec sheets, 159–160

B

back-end engineering with domain model, 88
Baker, Mark, 42, 173
Barker, Deane, 142
BBC Wildlife Finder, 9, 133–134, 183, 196, 203
Berners-Lee, Tim, 26, 192, 209
boundary objects, 84–85
breakpoints, 179
Budd, Andy, 66

C

camel case, 71
card sorts, 58
cardinality of domain objects, 80–84
　1:1 relationships, 81
　1:*n* relationships, 81, 82–83
　m:n relationships, 81–83
　recursive relationships, 83–84
categorizing subject domains, 47–48
choreography in IA, 208
chunks
　advantages of, 34
　chunking layout-based elements, 136
　creating domain model from, 84
　designing content with, 128–132, 133–135
　making templates from resource, 128–132
　optimal size for, 133–135
　organizing into structured content, 40
　responsive layouts and, 179
　URLs as, 129
CMS (content management systems)
　advantages of single-topic resources, 123–126

CMS (*continued*)
    converting content type to, 150–152
    creating collections in, 183–184
    customizing roles and permissions
      in, 146
    entity reference data types specs, 157
    entity-based CMS systems, 144–145
    headless CMS systems, 146
    HTML templates implemented
      in, 175–178
    implementing connected content
      with, 142–143
    object relationships in, 71–72
    planning future content and
      design, 19–20
    proprietary systems, 147
    sustaining growing, 18–19
    third-party system integration
      capability in, 146
    types of, 143–147
    viewing content as data, 4
    WordPress as, 147
    WYSIWYG editors as, 149
collaboration. *See also* teams
    developing collaborative mental
      models, 58–59
    encouraging group, 25
    making content models with, 101
collections, 183–184
communications team, 163
companies. *See* organizations
concepts. *See also* reusability; terms and
  definitions
    connecting from subject domain, 68–71
    defined, 33
    developing domain objects as
      reusable, 78
    promoting structure content, 28,
      204–207
connected content. *See* designing
  connected content
content. *See also* designing connected
  content; subject domains
    auditing, 132–133, 137
    authoring using structured, 40–41

benefits of domain modeling on, 27, 29
bottom-up approach to
  structuring, 15–16
changing faster, 25–26
creating structured, 137–138
curating, 182–184
as data, 4
defined, 33
design principles for, 118–120
designing for your audience, 24
developing shared vocabulary for, 66
domain research as foundation
  for, 64–65
format vs. type of, 98
function in domain model, 98
helping people find, 21
increasing ROI for, 22
linking data in, 209–210
planning before creating, 19–20
preparing for new technology, 21–22,
  201, 210–211
providing structure for future, 11, 117
readability of, 126–128
redundant, 27–28
reusing existing, 8–9, 20–21, 205
structured, 4–5, 32–33
in structured content stack, 169
subject domain as infrastructure
  for, 46–47
taxonomies inherent in, 158–159
template-based design for, 168–169
uncovering hidden, 138–139
usability testing for, 24
user-centered, 121
using responsive web design with, 179
working with troublesome, 135–137
content APIs, 194–196
Content Design (Richards), 118
content management systems. *See* CMS
content models
  adding content types to, 109
  advantages of structured, 140
  collaboration on, 101
  defined, 98
  deriving from domain models, 98–101

how they're used, 111–112
Priest on, 27–29
reconnecting content types to form, 110–111
in structured content stack, 169
Tong on, 113–114
content spec sheets, 159–160
content strategists, 164
content strategy
  domain models used for, 88
  implementing successfully, 207–208
  structured content as basis for, 42
content types
  adding to content models, 109
  applying taxonomies to, 157–159
  attributes for, 103–106
  combining domain objects in, 106–109
  conversion of domain objects to, 102
  converting from content model to CMS, 150–152
  defined, 33, 98
  developing, 102–103
  implementing in CMS, 148–157
  index comprising, 188
  reconnecting into content model, 110–111
  single-topic resources for, 123–126
contextual inquiry, 52
contextual navigation, 186, 187, 189–190
costs
  domain modeling impact on, 29
  reducing with structured content, 204–206
  ROI for content, 22
"create once, publish everywhere" (COPE) process, 27, 114, 147
creating domain models, 67–95
  agreeing on your domain, 76–77
  back-end engineering, 88
  building relationships between objects, 71–72
  chunking model, 84
  connecting concepts from subject domain, 68–71
  content strategy, 88
  designating domain objects for, 69–70

developing good domain objects, 77–79
discovering boundary objects, 84–85
finding ubiquitous language, 80
involving experts in, 85–87
live music, 90–91
modeling for future, 91–92
relationships in IA Summit domain model, 72–74
restaurants, 89–90
Smethurst on, 93–95
sticky note method for, 74–76
teamwork in, 74, 76
theme park domain model, 88–89
uses for models, 87–91
CSS (cascading style sheets), 178, 180

D

Darwin Information Typing Architecture (DITA), 42
data types
  CMS field specs for IA Summit, 152–154
  entity reference, 155–157
DDD (domain-driven design) sessions, 93–95
De Vries, Ellen, 66
design. *See also* future-friendly design; redesign cycle; teams
  agreeing on structure first, 10–11
  bottom-up approach to, 15–16
  cycle of redesign, 18–19, 22
  defining, 10
  making faster changes to, 25–26
  navigation and URL design, 191–194
  planning ahead for content and, 19–20
  reorganizing content into new, 20–21
  structure and, 9–10
designers
  role in implementation team, 163
  uncovering hidden content, 138–139
designing connected content, 117–140
  advantages of structured content models, 140
  auditing content, 132–133, 137
  chunking, 128–132, 133–135
  constructing content resources, 120

designing connected content (*continued*)
  creating new content, 137–138
    focusing resources on single
      topic, 123–126
    linking to other sources, 139
    planning priorities, 138
    principles for content, 118–120
    publishing only what you have, 139–140
    Ranganathan's laws of library
      science, 121
    structuring for readability, 126–128
    terms related to, 33
    transclusion, 176
    uncovering hidden content, 138–139
    using responsive layouts, 179
    Wikipedia's method for, 122–123, 139
    working with troublesome
      content, 135–137
device strategies
    designing interfaces using, 170
    using responsive layouts, 179
display templates, 128–132
distinctiveness of content, 119–120
DITA (Darwin Information Typing
  Architecture), 42
domain models. *See also* creating
  domain models
    benefits of, 29
    creating for future, 91–92
    deriving content models from, 98–101
    function of, 98
    getting started with, 27–29
    IA Summit website, 72–74, 99, 102,
      106, 107, 203
    integrating into projects, 28–29
    live music, 90–91
    organic growth of, 29
    relationship to content models, 98
    restaurant, 89–90
    reusing IA Summit, 203
    revising relationships between domain
      objects, 73
    running sessions for, 93–95
    in structured content stack, 169
    theme park, 88–89
    uses for, 87–91

domain objects. *See also* relationships
  attributes of, 77–78, 79, 103–106
  auditing content mapping to, 133
  cardinality of, 80–84
  combining in content type, 106–109
  converting to content types, 102
  defined, 68–69
  designating, 69–70
  developing, 77–79
  finding boundary objects, 84–85
  global navigation using, 187
  instances vs., 70
  number of attributes for, 107
  relationships between, 71–72, 73
  relevancy of, 100
  selecting for content model, 99–101
  sticky note creation of, 74–76
domain-drive design (DDD) sessions, 93–95
Domain-Driven Design (Evans), 68
domains, 33

E

Eames, Charles, 120
engineering landmarks, 35–40
engineers, 163
entities
    defined, 33, 155
    flexible structuring for, 41
entity-based CMS systems, 144
Evans, Eric, 68
Every Page Is Page One (Baker), 42, 173
experts. *See* SMEs

F

findable content, 119
five laws of library science, 121
flexibility, 34, 41
focused content, 119
forms, 136
front-end developer, 163
Frost, Brad, 180
Fuller, Buckminster, 210
future-friendly design
    anticipating new technology, 21–22,
      201, 210–211
    cost savings of, 204–206

creating future domain models, 91–92
designing for multiple
    platforms, 194–196
developing team for, 206–207
implementation successes for, 207–208
linking data in content for, 209–210
planning for, 19–20
promoting structured content, 28,
    203–207
revamping IA Summit website, 202–203
structure for, 11, 117

G

games and interactives, 136
Gibson, William, 209
global navigation, 186, 187, 188–189
Golden Gate Bridge web page, 35–37
governance of structured content
    documenting, 159, 160
    on websites, 203–204

H

Hall, Erika, 64
headless CMS systems, 146
Hemingway, Ernest, 32
Historical Civil Engineering
    Landmarks, 35–40
HTML documents
    adding attributes to basic template, 176
    creating basic resource template,
        175–178
    JASON files vs., 195
    styling with CSS, 178, 180
    testing usability of page design, 178

I

IA (information architecture), 14–16,
    208–209
IA Summit website
    composing session template
        for, 129–132
    content types for, 145–146, 150
    converting content types to
        CMS, 150–152
    current design of, 202–203

data types for CMS field specs, 152–154
domain model for, 72–74, 99, 102,
    106, 107
expert interviews for, 52–57
final content model for, 110–111
global navigation for, 188–189
objects for, 69–72
possible authoring interface for,
    126–128
redesigning website, 14–15
reusing domain model, 203
Session content type, 108–109,
    150–152, 154
speaker index for, 181
templates for, 171–173, 181
working with entity reference data
    types, 155–157
implementing connected content.
    See also CMS; navigation
    about, 165
    assembling team for, 162–164
    CMS needed for, 142–143
    creating content spec sheets, 159–160
    designing mobile apps, 194–196
    entering content in system, 160–161
    getting started, 142
    implementing content types
        in CMS, 148–157
    navigation, 185–194
    reusable templates for, 197
    taxonomies for, 157–159
    types of CMS used, 143–147
    web content management
        systems, 143–146
    web publishing systems for, 143
improving content faster, 25–26
index templates
    bottom-up approach to, 180–182
    contextualizing resources
        with, 171–173
indexes
    collections, 183–184
    comprised of content type, 188
    content curation with, 182–184
    IA Summit website speaker, 181
informal communications, 94, 95

information architecture (IA), 14–16,
208–209
instances
arranging for structured content, 38–39
defined, 33
domain objects vs., 70
interface design
adding CSS to HTML documents,
178, 180
basic HTML resource template, 175–178
coding or mocking up
templates for, 171
devising device strategies, 170
domain model uses for, 87
future technology for, 210–211
planning templates, 171–173
stack of structured content, 169
template-based design, 168–169
timing for, 6
Interviewing Users (Portigal), 64
interviews
experts, 50–58
target users, 59–61
inverted pyramid, 173

J

JSON (JavaScript Object Notation), 195
Just Enough Research (Hall), 64

K

Klyn, Dan, 208

L

layers of structured content, 169
leadership, 163–164
Lineup content type, 156–157
live music models
content model, 100–101
domain model, 90–91

M

Marcotte, Ethan, 179
marketing team, 163
measuring success, 207–208

metadata
assigning to chunks, 34
defined, 33
taxonomies inherent in, 158–159
Metadata Basics for Web Content
(Andrews), 42
mobile apps, 194–196
model-based navigation, 185
models. *See also* content models; domain
models
building CMS to fit, 147
defined, 33

N

National Public Radio (NPR), 147
navigation
contextual, 186, 187, 189–190
global, 186, 187
model-based, 185
redirecting website, 193
in structured content stack, 169
URL design for, 191–194
Nelson, Ted, 176, 211
Niebuhr, Reinhold, 211
non-profit's use of content model, 113–114

O

objects. *See also* domain objects
boundary, 84–85
defined, 33
one-to-many (1:*n*) relationships, 81
one-to-one (1:1) relationships, 81
ontology, 208
optional relationships, 83
organizations. *See also* stakeholders; teams
developing content cooperatively, 21
governance of structured content, 159,
160, 203–204
integrating domain modeling into
projects, 28–29
introducing future-friendly design to,
203–204
leadership in, 163–164
learning about culture of, 93–94, 95
objections to research within, 61–64

P

Performer content type, 156, 157
photo galleries and carousels, 135
Portigal, Steve, 64
Priest, Annette, 27–29
product manager, 163
project manager, 163
projects. *See also* teams
　assembling teams for, 162–164
　developing website using content
　　model, 113–114
　entering Civil Engineering
　　Landmarks, 39
　integrating domain modeling
　　into, 28–29
properties. *See* attributes
proprietary CMS systems, 147
pull quotes and callouts, 136

R

Rand, Paul, 10
Ranganathan, Siyali Ramamrita, 121
readability of content, 126–128
recording interviews, 52
recursive relationships, 83–84
redesign cycle
　avoiding, 205
　conventional phases in, 18–19
　focusing on visual changes in, 22
　redesigning IA Summit website, 14–16
redirecting website navigation, 193
redundant content, 27–28
references, 155
relationships
　1:1, 81
　1:*n*, 81, 82–83
　m:n, 81–83
　building, 71–72
　cardinality for, 80–84
　drawing, 75
　entity reference data types, 155–157
　optional, 83
　recursive, 83–84
　revising, 73
representation, 33, 169

researching subject domains
　defining problems while, 64–65
　importance of, 45, 50
　overcoming objections to, 61–64
　using existing research, 60–61
resources
　amount of content needed for, 138
　basic HTML template for, 175–178
　constructing content, 120
　contextualizing with index
　　templates, 172–173
　defined, 33, 171
　focusing on single topic, 123–126
　making templates from chunks
　　of, 128–132
　referencing in URLs, 192
　selecting for template design, 171–173
　structure connecting content, 6
Responsive Web Design (Marcotte), 179
restaurant domain models, 89–90
reusability
　avoiding redesign cycles, 205
　becoming future friendly, 11
　borrowing domain models, 203
　designing structure to reuse
　　content, 8–9
　developing reusable domain objects, 78
　improving content faster, 25–26
　reusing existing content, 8–9,
　　20–21, 205
　scalability and single-topic
　　resources, 125
　working with reusable templates, 197
Richards, Sarah, 118
ROI for content, 22
Rumsfeld, Donald, 49

S

scalability, 125
scheduling
　domain modeling sessions, 94–95
　SME interview sessions, 53–54
Schema.org, 210
Scott, Tom, 133–134, 203
search engines, 21

sensemaking, 6
Session content type, 108–109, 150–152, 154
Sharon, Tomer, 49
sidebar infobox, 189–190
"Simple Things Make Firm Foundations"
    (Berners-Lee), 26
single-topic resources, 123–126
smartphone apps, 194–197
SMEs (subject-matter experts). *See also*
    SME interviews
        defined, 50
        detailed knowledge on subject
            domain, 60
        gleaning terms from, 57–58
        interviewing, 50–58
        involving in domain model creation,
            85–87, 93–95
        learning about content structure
            from, 7
        user views vs. views of, 60
SME interviews, 50–58
    card sorts to aid, 58
    compiling terms and definitions
        from, 57–58
    conducting, 52–57
    mapping mental models of, 58–59
    preparation for, 51–52
    recording, 52
Smethurst, Michael, 93–95
speaker index, 181
spreadsheets
    aiding in content model design, 113
    auditing content from, 132
    model implementation using, 142
    tracking content types in, 148, 149, 161
stack of structured content, 169
stakeholders
    aligning, 101
    contacting, 23
    engaging, 86, 164
    overcoming objections of, 61–64
    sharing domain research with, 65
sticky note method, 74–76
storytelling, 93
structure, 34

structured content
    advantages of, 140
    applying to existing pages, 35–37
    arranging instances for, 38–39
    becoming future friendly, 11
    bottom-up approach to, 15–16
    breaking into parts, 35
    content strategy based on, 42
    defined, 32–33
    designing structure, 6–7
    effect on writing content, 40–41
    flexibility of, 34
    organizing chunks into, 40
    overview, 4–5
    promoting, 28, 204–207
    readability as goal for, 126–128
    reusing existing content, 8–9
    stacks in, 169
    teamwork required for, 10–11
subject domains
    about, 6
    categorizing, 47–48
    contacting target users about, 59–61
    creating domain model from, 68–71
    existing research on, 60–61
    experts vs. users on, 60
    exploring, 48–49
    interviewing experts in, 50–58
    overcoming objections to research
        on, 61–64
    providing infrastructure for
        content, 46–47
    researching, 45, 50
    target user interviews about, 59–61
    uncovering domain complexity, 66
    UX research vs. domain
        research, 64–65
subject-matter experts. *See* SMEs

T

tables, 136
target users. *See* users
targeted content, 119
taxonomies, 157–159, 208

teams
    agreement on domain, 76–77
    chunking parts of domain model, 84
    clarifying subject domain
       complexity, 66
    collaboration among, 25, 58–59, 101
    contacting stakeholders, 23
    creating domain models, 74, 76
    deriving content models from domain
       models, 98–101
    designing structure first, 10–11
    developing, 23
    developing future-friendly content,
       206–207
    domain-driven design by, 93–95
    exploring subject domains, 48–49
    finding ubiquitous language, 80
    implementing CMS systems, 162–164
    making good domain objects, 77–79
    planning content priorities, 138
    running domain modeling
       sessions, 93–95
technology of the future, 21–22, 201, 210–211
templates
    arranging Civil Engineering
       Landmarks, 38–40
    basic HTML resource, 175–178
    coding or mocking up interface, 171
    composing IA Summit session, 129–132
    content spec sheet, 159–160
    developing from content model
       attributes, 128–132
    index templates, 171–173, 180–182
    planning, 171–173
    usefulness of, 132
    using for interface design, 168–169
terms and definitions
    finding ubiquitous language, 80
    gleaning from experts, 57–58
    learning from user analytics, 61
    related to connected content, 33
    vocabulary dump techniques, 66
theme park domain model, 88–89
third-party system integration
  capability, 146

Tong, Josh, 113–114
Top Trumps card game, 103–105
transclusion, 176

U

ubiquitous language, 80
uncovering hidden content, 138–139
URI (uniform resource identifier), 194
URLs (uniform resource locators)
    chunks as, 129
    designing for websites, 191–194
    URIs vs., 194
usability
    designing content for usefulness
       and, 118–119
    testing apps for, 24
user experience. *See* UX
users. *See also* audience
    customizing roles and permissions
       for, 146
    designing CMSs for, 148–149
    focusing subject domain issues, 60
    improving service to, 205
    interviewing, 59–61
    learning terminology of, 61
    linking web content to domain
       for, 173–174
    testing page designs with, 178
uses for domain models, 87–91
UX (user experience)
    content design with, 118–120
    UX research vs. domain
       research, 64–65

V

vocabulary dump technique, 66

W

Web Content Management (Barker), 142
web content management systems, 143–146
web publishing systems, 143, 147
Webb, Eileen, 148

websites. *See also* designing connected
content; IA Summit website
  content models as basis for, 113
  encouraging group collaboration for, 25
  global navigation for, 188–189
  how content fits wider world, 26
  learning users' terms for, 61
  maintenance and single-topic
    resources, 125
  multiple entry points to, 173–174
  ongoing governance of structured
    content on, 203–204
  publishing what you have, 139–140
  redirecting navigation on, 193
  site maps vs. domain models, 68
  structuring existing pages, 35–37
  URL design for, 191–194
  URL vs. URI, 194
  Wikipedia, 122–123, 139, 189–190

Wikipedia, 122–123, 139, 189–190
Wildlife Finder, 9, 133–134, 183, 196, 203
WordPress, 147
writers. *See* authors
writing content
  using content spec sheets, 159–160
  using structured approach, 40–41
WYSIWYG (what you see is what you get)
  editors, 149

X

XML (Extensible Markup Language), 42